# Rethinking Islam
# and Liberal Democracy

# Rethinking Islam and Liberal Democracy

## Islamist Women in Turkish Politics

Yeşim Arat

*State University of New York Press*

Published by
State University of New York Press, Albany

For information, address State University of New York Press,
194 Washington Avenue, Suite 305, Albany, NY 12210-2365

Production by Marilyn P. Semerad
Marketing by Michael Campochiaro

**Library of Congress Cataloging-in-Publication Data**

Arat, Yeşim, 1955–
    Rethinking Islam and liberal democracy : Islamist women in Turkish
politics / Yeşim Arat.
      p. cm.
    Includes bibliographical references and index.
    ISBN 0-7914-6465-2 (hardcover : alk. paper)
    1. Women in politics—Turkey. 2. Muslim women—Political activity.
3. Refah Partisi (Turkey). 4. Political parties—Turkey. 5. Islam and
politics—Turkey. 6. Turkey—Politics and government. I. Title.

HQ1236.5.T9A733 2005
305.42'09561—dc22                                                  2004017001


10 9 8 7 6 5 4 3 2 1

FOR ZEYNEP AND ŞEVKET

# Contents

# Acknowledgments

This book began as a study of Islamist women's associations in Turkey. It was part of a larger work on political Islam carried out under the auspices of the Turkish Economic and Social Studies Foundation, TESEV. Binnaz Toprak proposed the larger project and invited me to undertake the section on Islamist women. Thanks to her compelling proposal, the project was generously supported by TESEV. I am grateful to Binnaz Toprak for asking me to work on this issue, which I enjoyed immensely. Had she not extended her offer, this book would not have been conceived. I would also like to thank TESEV for its financial support. Deniz Erkmen and Selma Sabanoviç, my students at the time, worked as my assistants and helped me with the interviews. They were bright, reliable. Ayşegül Karayazgan and Ruşen Çakır helped me arrange my initial interviews.

Even though I toyed with the idea of using my research to develop it into a book, the "realm of necessity" asserted itself and obstructed the realization of the idea. It was at this point that Müge Göçek intervened and changed things. Not only did she help me arrange for a sabbatical at the University of Michigan, Center for Middle Eastern and North African Studies so that I would work on the book but she adamantly believed, more than I did, that I would write it. Her unswerving faith gave me the stamina to finalize the book. Margot Badran read the entire manuscript and came up with concrete proposals for the publication of the book, which, though not actualized, kept me going. My two readers at the State University of New York Press provided sound criticism. Their advice and guidance was invaluable. Dina LeGall, Deniz Kandiyoti, and Amy Singer each gave me precious advice regarding publication. Friends or colleagues graciously invited me to present various portions of the draft in various academic gatherings, including the University of Michigan, The Rockefeller Foundation Bellagio Center, University of Berkeley, Tel Aviv University, Yale University, and Princeton University, all helping me to develop my thesis. My husband, Şevket Pamuk, read the draft and pushed me—

with his customary, exacting standards—to sharpen my thoughts. He was the first and last reader. My daughter, Zeynep Pamuk, was my closest ally, encouraging me to work on the manuscript and even helping with the notes. I am most grateful for all the support I received. The women and men I interviewed from the Refah and Fazilet Parties made the book possible by sharing their lives and their views with me. I thank them all very much.

# Introduction

This book is based on a study of the women activists of the Islamist Refah (Welfare) Party in Turkey.[1] The women's organizations of Refah were established in 1989, six years after the party was founded, and closed in 1998 along with the party by a constitutional court decision.[2] In their short life span, these organizations played a critical role both in bringing their party to power and engaging a large female constituency in politics. Hundreds of women were working for the party and recruiting thousands of others to support it. Refah received the highest percentage of votes in the 1995 elections (21.4 percent) and was the major partner of the governing coalition from June 1996 to July 1997. For the first time in Turkish political life, a religiously inspired political party had come to power. Moreover, Refah had an impact in politics as the precursor of the Adalet ve Kalkınma (Justice and Development) Party. Adalet ve Kalkınma came to power after the November 2002 elections as a single-party government after a period of coalitions going back to 1991.

If "the locus of study is not the object of study," as Clifford Geertz reminds us,[3] then the Ladies' Commissions of the Refah Party is only the locus of my work. Within this locus, I try to understand the women activists of the Refah Party using qualitative methods, primarily via in-depth interviews. I trace who the women activists of the commissions were, how they were recruited into politics in the Islamist camp, how they recruited other women to vote for their party, and what their worldviews were.

The object of my work, however, is broader. Through this study, I examine the conflictual relationship between secularism and Islam in a liberal democracy. Islam versus liberal democracy, and secularism versus Islam have long been linked as antithetical. This antithetical positioning conceals the extent to which these concepts can be part of one another in historically specific contexts. I trace this interdependence through the experiences of the people who live by them. Refah women challenged the preconceived attributes that the secular establishment

1

projected to Islamism, and they negotiated with ingenuity what Islam can entail in a secular democratic polity. They redefined what liberal individualism can or should accommodate in a secular context. Through their experience, we can assess how religion can assume new meanings, threaten or expand the boundaries of secular democracy, and reshape socio-political reality. We can explore how liberalism that prioritizes the individual and his or her human rights can transform, coexist, or remain in tension with a belief system that allegedly prioritizes a collective notion of identity in which a sacred God legitimizes rights. Boundaries of Islam are porous, and liberalism infiltrates these boundaries. I maintain that liberal democracy could enrich itself by accommodating these groups rather than excluding them.

The antithetical positioning between Islam and liberal democracy has important implications for contemporary debates on illiberal challenges to liberal democracies.[4] Problems of accommodating so-called communitarian religions in secular liberal democracies trouble many culturally diverse societies. Practical problems in dealing with headscarved Muslim girls in schools or with polygamous marriages carried out according to Islamic precepts persist in many established liberal democracies of the West and challenge their prevailing citizenship laws.

Under these conditions, on the one hand, contemporary political theorists reconsider and expand the parameters of liberalism to make it more amenable to cultural diversity. They emphasize the importance of culture for the individual. Culture promotes human well-being, because it cultivates a community and a feeling of belonging. It is also the medium in which meaningful individual choice and autonomy can be sought.[5] Even though blueprints to accommodate cultural diversity are difficult to sustain, theorists rethink liberalism to integrate group rights to enhance the civil and political rights of the individual.

On the other hand, the "clash of civilizations" thesis resurfaces and reverberates. Even though many refuted Samuel Huntington's thesis[6] for its simplistic and essentialist depiction of cultures and cultural interaction, his conceptual framework proved its resilience, particularly with the September 11, 2001 terrorist attacks. Islam quickly became the inscrutable, violent, and intractable Other, a threat to liberal democratic values.

This essentialist reading of Islam does not take place only in the West. In the secular but Muslim Turkish context, the controversy was redefined among those who claimed to prioritize a certain understanding of secularism as opposed to others who claimed to prioritize a certain Islamist identity. The "secularists" feared the gradually spreading wave of "Islamism" and the Islamist claims to political power through the parliamentary system. The "Islamists" resented this fear. The "secularists" assumed that Islamists were all authoritarian, illiberal reactionaries, and the "Islamists" believed the secularists to be the same. This exclusionary polarization foreclosed dialogue and mystified the claims of each side. Polarization denied the recognition of either interchange between or transformation within different belief systems. Edward Said, in his criticism of Huntington and the clash of civilizations thesis, argued that the history of civilizations was not only one of "wars of religion and imperial conquest but also one of exchange, cross-fertilization and sharing."[7] It is this exchange, cross-fertilization, and sharing between Islamists and their secular adversaries that I trace in this book. An awareness of this interconnection might provide a critical perspective on the problems of accommodating seemingly irreconcilable belief systems such as liberalism and Islam. In real life, neither ideology may be as pure and categorical as its respective adherents tend to assume.

## SECULARISM AND ISLAM IN A DEMOCRATIC STATE

The Turkish context is unique if we want to probe into the dynamic relationship between Islam and secularism. The contemporary Turkish Republic inherited a Muslim Ottoman culture and a predominantly Muslim population when it was established in 1923. The founding elite and its single-party regime then opted for a project of modernization à la West that was defined primarily by its secularizing measures.[8] Cultivation of secularism rather than democracy became a priority. The project of modernization and its secularizing measures were in tension with Islam, because the state aimed to privatize religion, thus redefining what it was and where it belonged.

Before the establishment of the Republic, Islam helped legitimize the patriarchal Ottoman rule and the secular authority the sultans had to control religion. The Republic, however, severed all ties with the religiously sanctioned Ottoman Empire to become a secular Westernizing nation-state.[9] The first article of the 1921 constitution declared that sovereignty belonged to the nation unconditionally, thus replacing Islam as a principle of political legitimacy.

The founding fathers initiated a series of institutional and legal reforms to disestablish Islam and separate religious institutions of the state from those of society.[10] The caliphate was abolished. Similar fates befell the position of the Şeyh-ül-Islam (the highest Muslim authority of the Ottoman state) and the ministry of religious foundations. In their place, the General Directorate of Religious Affairs and the General Directorate of Pious Foundations were instituted. The Law on the Unity of Education outlawed religious education and established state control over education. In 1926, a new civil code was adopted from the Swiss code. The new code, which was critical for providing the framework of male female equality in the polity, unequivocally dismantled the power of the Shariat, the Muslim law, over political and social life.

A conspicuous desire not merely to disestablish Islam but also to control it was manifest in the secularization process of the founding fathers. The General Director of Religious Affairs, the highest religious authority in the country responsible for the administration of all mosques, was appointed by the President and worked under the Prime Minister. The Directorate decided unilaterally on what was to be published on or related to religion and was the formal legal authority on religious questions. The state thus aimed to supervise religious observance, its content, and the limits within which it could be practiced.

Controlling Islam and its role in people's lives was pursued not merely at the formal or legal level but also at the popular level. The brotherhoods, religious orders, convents, and sanctuaries were closed, which severed the organic links that the mass of the population had to popular Islam in the public domain. The traditional fez associated with male Islamic dress codes was banned and replaced by Western-style hats. The call to prayer traditionally delivered from the minarets in Arabic was translated and delivered in Turkish. In the words of Bernard Lewis, "The state aimed to end the power of organized Islam and break its hold on the minds and hearts of the Turkish people."[11]

Thus, secularism, in its inception, was intimately linked to state authority. The founding fathers were heroic commanders who had won a war of independence, but their hard-won legitimacy could not change the fact that they ran the country with a single party regime until 1950. An authoritarian, single-party regime had initiated and instituted the secularizing reforms at the cost of democratization.

The process of democratization in the country, in turn, was intimately linked to relaxing state control over religious life. The emergence of the Democrat Party in 1946 heralded the initial signs of this change. The Democrat Party promised democracy, and this meant, at least in part, allowing more scope for religious expression in public life. When Democrats came to power in 1950, they immediately allowed the call to prayer to be delivered in Arabic. They opened Prayer

Leader and Preacher schools and tried to appease the people's desire for public religious observance.

As the country developed and demands for further democratization became inevitable, the first Islamist political party, Milli Nizam (National Order) Party, emerged in 1970. It was duly closed by a constitutional court order, which claimed that the party exploited religion and threatened secularism, thereby violating the constitution. The closed party was soon to be followed by its replacement, the Milli Selamet (National Salvation) Party. The new party upheld traditional values and drew attention to the significance of history in communal life. Soon, the Milli Selamet Party became an articulate critic of modernization à la Westernization, which repressed and denied the role of religion in people's lives.

After the 1980 military intervention, the Islamist Refah Party was founded to uphold the heritage of the Milli Nizam Party and insist on the pursuit of a "moral order." Unlike its predecessor, which had played a key role in the coalition governments of the 1970s but remained a minor party, the Refah Party became the major opposition party in the country and then—following the 1995 elections in which it received the largest percentage of votes—the major coalition partner in government. In its 1993 convention, the Refah Party expounded the system of "multiple legal orders" and the freedom of the citizens to choose the legal order, which would allow them to live by their beliefs.[12] The Refah Party took a proposal to parliament to amend the principle of secularism, which, it claimed, was inadequate to meet the demands of the day. The initiative failed but was indicative of the demands articulated by the Refah Party. They declared that the notion of secularism, which was one of the fundamental principles of the Republic, was insufficient to accommodate the needs of a major portion of the population.

The process of secularization and the Islamist challenge to its particular unfolding led to a serious polarization within society. There were those who were for the kind of secularism initiated by the founding fathers, and there were the Islamist "others" who opposed it. Each side became deeply suspicious of the other, as values became entrenched over time.[13] The small secular constituency that criticized Republican secularism and the tight state control over religion was not strong enough to dissipate the polarization or bridge the gap. The military memorandum that precipitated the fall of the Refah Party government from power and the consequent closure of the party was given in this context of polarization and reflected its tension.

## COMMUNITARIAN VALUES AND INDIVIDUALISM

The confrontation between secularists and Islamists and the projections each side made toward the other were multi layered. The secularists feared Islamists not only because they suspected the latter of disintegrating the Republic but also because the Islamists were considered to be illiberal communitarians. The new Republic had initiated a project of modernization and endorsed Western values. The modernizing state aimed to shed traditional norms associated with Islam and adopt liberal Western values, including secularism and individualism. On the other hand, Islamists resented the imposition of Western norms, including a disdain for communitarian Islamist morals that the project of modernization necessitated. They accused secularists of reckless, self-seeking individualism. However, the stigma of individualism associated with the modernist seculars and communitarianism with the traditional Islamists was complicated.

If liberalism was at the core of Western civilization, and if liberalism was an ethic of individualism, the Turkish project of Westernization lacked both. The notion of the West was redefined in the Turkish context. Communitarian values that had primarily defined the Ottoman tradition that preceded the Republic were perpetuated through a different, namely, solidarist nationalist discourse within the republic. The tradition of a strong patrimonial state that could enforce its will, at least to gather taxes and conscript soldiers, allowed a communitarian view of society to be enforced with ease. Metin Heper called the Turkish state a "transcendental" one in which the rulers know the best interest of the ruled, exercised power for the people, at times despite the people, because of the legitimacy its communitarian ideology had.[14] Consequently, the transition from communitarian Islamism to communitarian nationalism was smooth. In pursuit of their mission for civilizational transformation, the founding elite could not and did not respect liberal values that prioritized the value of the individual and self-expression. Recognizing the need for self-expression would have meant accommodating opposition. Yet, the new regime was not entrenched enough to confront the challenge. Breaking the hold of religion was seen as the primary condition of westernization, even if this involved autocratic means. In this process, liberalism was left for future generations to grapple with.

The founding elite, instead of nurturing political liberalism, propagated a nationalist ideology that upheld communitarian values. The individual was important to the extent that he or she contributed to the national community, which was assumed to be a homogenous whole.

The principle of populism, which came to mean "for the people, at times despite the people," allowed for collectivist norms to define Turkish nationalism. Consequently, Islamic solidarity, which defined the basis of the political community, was replaced by a nationalist solidarity.

Going back to the Young Turks—the Ottoman precursors of the Republican regime—authoritarian, communitarian norms that ignored the individual prevailed among Turkish nationalists.[15] It was Ahmet Rıza and his pro-centralization, communitarian, elitist ideas that left their imprint both on Young Turk thought and rule, as opposed to Prince Sabahattin and his liberalism advocating some type of decentralization and individual initiative within the polity. Young Turk rule was characterized by a rule from above shaped by the ascendance of military and bureaucratic elites who were skeptical of the common people.

The tradition of respect for individual rights and individual initiative was still weak and inarticulate. After the Republic was formed, there were groups who were wary of the founder of the nation Atatürk's increasing authoritarianism.[16] Yet, their opposition was never articulated with reference to explicit liberal norms. The short-lived opposition parties of the single-party era, Progressive Republican Party (1924–25), and later the Free Republican Party (1930), prioritized protection of religion in their opposition to authoritarianism, rather than demands for democratic participation and respect for civil liberties, concepts not particularly popular at the time. With the advent of the Democrat Party, political liberalism became an issue, but when in power the Democrats themselves resorted to authoritarianism. The proliferation of political parties and the emergence of Islamist parties did not change the trend. Islamist parties advocated extending the realm of religion within public life and religious freedoms of the individual, but their respect for liberalism as a doctrine, which necessitated respect not only for their devout constituency but all others, was never articulated. In short, the communitarian tradition always lurked behind liberal rhetoric in the Turkish polity. Liberalism was an aspiration fueled by this confrontation. In the contemporary period, Islamists were easily labeled as illiberal by the secular modernists whose liberal credentials were also suspect.

## WHY WOMEN

To understand the changing dynamics of secularism and Islam in contemporary Turkey, this study will focus on women of the Refah Party. Focusing on women is important, because both the project of modernity and any alternative Islamist discourse has been defined and continue to define themselves over the roles and status ascribed to women.[17] Confrontation between the liberals and Islamists takes place over the rights and responsibilities or dress codes of women. Ironically, even though the modernist secular state radically expanded women's opportunities and status in society, women were marginalized in political life and in party politics. On the other hand, even though most common understandings of Islam recognize various restrictions and impediments to women's claim to "power," including seclusion and priority given to maternal roles, women's return to Islam seem to have been an important catalyst for their increased political participation.

Women's organization and activism in the Refah Party was an unprecedented phenomenon. No other party in Turkey could boast a similar membership of women. Refah Party women registered close to one million women members in about six years. Refah Party men claimed that women were instrumental in persuading many husbands to register with the party. Observers of the party argued that the women's organizations were perhaps the most dynamic unit of the party, visible in all its rallies, meetings, and activities.[18] The press duly recognized the activism of the organization with captions such as "The dynamo of the Refah Party in the elections are women,"[19] "Refah Party women are the most industrious,"[20] and "Ladies of the Refah Party are like bees,"[21] and referred to the president of the Istanbul organization as "The Refah Party woman who carried Tayyip to the Mayoralty."[22] Other parties, consequently, tried to adopt similar methods of mobilizing women to draw votes.[23]

Even though much has been written on the Refah Party in general and the significance of the Islamist revival it helped usher onto the Turkish political scene,[24] its female activists and the ladies' commission of the party, or "Refah Partisi Hanımlar Komisyonu" as they have been called in Turkish, have not been a focus of extensive research. Journalists and reporters, not merely those of the Refah Party ranks but in the secular press as well, have shown due interest and reported on the visible activism of the Refah Party women. Interviews with members of the ladies' commissions have been carried in daily newspapers,[25] but there is more to know about these women to apprehend the dynamics of change they precipitated in both the Islamist and secular ranks. How do these women carve their Islamic identity? In private as well as political contexts, how is this identity used to renegotiate power? What does it mean to assume an Islamic self and live Islamic lives in a secular context? Do they partake in political decision-making more equally than they did before, or do they become hostage to a new set of circumstances in which a male elite operates in the name of their sacred beliefs? How is an appeal to Islam reconciled with demands of political participation in a democracy? Does the process expand parameters of democratic politics in Turkey? As Islamist party workers, do they become more empowered individuals or merely more successful appendages of their newly defined community? How do their activities shape the role and meaning of religion in Turkish democracy? These questions have implications for negotiating the boundaries of liberal democracies.

I was drawn to the Refah Party ladies' commissions, because of their apparent success and in order to explore what lay behind that success. As a student of politics long interested in questions of democracy and political participation, particularly political participation of women, I was struck with the political activism of Refah Party women. The intensity and extent of Refah women activists' engagement in politics was striking even beyond the Turkish context. It had long been argued that women lacked interest in politics. Even though feminist literature clearly contested the claim and argued that women were more involved and interested in politics than the orthodox political scientists assumed,[26] women have not been militant activists in large numbers within the party ranks. Women have been known to support conservative causes (for example, the New Right in the United States) and to be actively involved in Islamist movements (such as the Iranian Revolution). However, in Turkey, there was an Islamist political party in a secular democratic polity through which women engaged in politics. Women, in less than a decade, helped carry the party—which was a marginal one in the late 1980s—to power, as the larger coalition partner of the government. Broader questions of power and identity had their tangible locus in these women.

Activism of Islamist women was particularly interesting, because Islamist politics was a highly charged issue in Turkey. As the number of women expressing themselves through an Islamic identity increased, the rift between them and the traditionally secular groups increased. The question remained as to what extent the polarization between "secular" as opposed to "Islamist" women was justified.

My research shows that women of the Refah Party crossed multiple boundaries as they worked to mobilize women in the private realm and move them into the political domain as voters and supporters of the party. They were women brought up in a secular context and they had adopted many of the values propagated by the secular Republic. As party workers, female activists mobilized other women through a process of apolitical politicization. In other words, both those who took part in the party organization and others who were recruited as members were politicized in the social context of person-alistic networks cultivated through neighborhood relations, which they carried into and preserved in the political domain. Party members successfully tapped the traditional mediums of socialization and po-liticized them. Even though they identified themselves as religious women, they appealed to the secular needs and aspirations of their constituency. They worked relentlessly for their Islamist party, be-cause their work satisfied their own worldly needs for achievement and recognition. They remained committed activists, because they derived personal/ individualistic satisfaction from the solidarity, com-radeship, and patriotism that their common engagement delivered above and beyond the emotional satisfaction of religious observance. Their success was a result of crossing the boundaries between the private and the political, secular and religious, democratic and au-thoritarian, and individualistic and communitarian. Their failures were defined by the boundaries they were unable to cross, such as the glass ceiling separating themselves from the men in their party.

## INTERVIEWS AND SURVEYS

This book is primarily based on intensive interviews conducted with Refah Party members. In addition to interviews, textual materials in-cluding secondary sources on the subject and primary material such as newspapers and publications of the Refah Party were surveyed. For the years 1994–1995, when the activities of the ladies' commissions were most intense, *Milli Gazete*, a daily that was closely linked to the Refah Party was surveyed. Interviews for the project were carried out from April to September 1998. In January 1998, the Refah Party was closed and its top leadership, including the charismatic chairman Necmettin Erbakan, was banned from politics for five years. Before the party was officially closed, Fazilet (Virtue) Party was launched to replace the Refah Party.[27] This was a period when the Islamists felt threatened and defensive. The party organization was dissipated, and the party members and archival material could not be reached as easily as would have been the case, had there been an intact organization.[28]

Interviewees were contacted through the snowballing method. Sibel Eraslan, who headed the Istanbul ladies' commission of the party between 1989 and 1994, and Ruşen Çakır, an expert on the Refah Party and the Islamist movement in Turkey, were the initial contacts. Eraslan had played an invaluable and critical role in the institutionalization and success of the ladies' commissions. Her reference and support helped me arrange many interviews that otherwise would have been impossible. Çakır knew Refah Party politics intimately and gave me the tips with which I reached the men in the party I wanted to interview. My affiliation with Boğaziçi University was an advantage in getting interviews, because the university had noticeably avoided violent confrontation in dealing with headscarved female students who were banned from universities. A total of twenty-four interviews, nineteen with women and five with men, were conducted. Of the nineteen women, fifteen were members of the ladies' commissions. An interview was carried out with an ex-Refah Party activist who was the president of the National Youth Foundation Women's Commission (Milli Gençlik Vakfı Kadın Komisyonu), that had organic links with the party and that was critical in cultivating young Refah Party sympathizers among women.

After the Refah Party was closed, the Fazilet Party appointed five women to the administrative bodies of its central party organization, a move that the Refah Party had not made. Of these five, three women were interviewed. Two of those interviewed were in the Central Decision and Executive Council (Merkez Karar ve Yürütme Kurulu) and one other in the consultative Party Council. One of the women in the Central Decision and Executive Council was also appointed to institutionalize the women's organization of the new party. Interviews with Fazilet Party members aimed to provide a perspective on the activities of the Refah Party women and trace the development of women's activism within the Islamist ranks in the early stages of the new party's institutionalization.

Ladies' commissions in the Refah Party were closely tied to the central organs of the party dominated by men. Men initiated the ladies' commissions and were responsible for educating women so that the latter could assume the task of institutionalization. A few men were interviewed to throw light on this process and to provide a perspective on the ladies' commissions from the central party administration.

Despite the advantages I had, such as being affiliated with the right institution and being able to connect with a venerable leader who was willing to help, securing interviews was not easy. Because the Refah Party organization had dissipated, simply contacting and locating people was difficult. The party was banned from politics by a court order, and women were hesitant to engage in any political act, including giving interviews. Women who denied interviews usually expressed their desire to consult colleagues, then declined afterward. Whether or not they actually consulted colleagues, the reference to the group was expected to give legitimacy to the refusal of the woman concerned. Group solidarity was important for the Refah Party women, and they expected I would understand them better when there was a collective inclination that giving an interview to someone who was not one of them was not quite right, particularly at the time the interview was requested. Men who had worked in the central party organs in Ankara could not be reached; phone calls were not returned, faxes went unanswered.

In Istanbul, it was easier to reach male members of the party. Men, including Tayyip Erdoğan, who was then the Mayor of the city and who had been responsible for initiating the ladies' commissions within the party in 1989, were responsive to my interview requests. Erdoğan, imprisoned after the closure of the Refah Party for cultivating religious separatism, was secure—as the Mayor of the largest city in Turkey—to talk about his party.

Interviews were carried out mostly in Istanbul, three in Ankara, and one in Bursa. The people who were interviewed were prominent leaders of their respective organizations. In the three cities, the presidents of the Refah Party provincial ladies' commissions could be interviewed. Others interviewed were either presidents of district organizations or those responsible from different branches of the ladies' commissions in the party. Men interviewed were well-known leaders of the Istanbul organization of the party.

Those who conceded to be interviewed gave their interviews with enthusiasm. Even when obtaining the interview was not easy, in the interview situation there was always a congenial atmosphere. Those who were ready to be interviewed aimed to make themselves better understood by the "other," the non-Islamist camp. This was an opportunity for propaganda or else, as one member put it, an opportunity "to make themselves understood by those who did not understand." Mostly, women preferred to be interviewed in their homes, men in their offices. Those interviewed were mostly of the middle class and had nuclear families with one or two children. In their homes, women always offered tea, coffee, or Coke along with cookies or cakes. Established boundaries were crossed and stereotypical images of Islamists were undermined when Coke was offered—a beverage Islamists discouraged their supporters to drink because it was a Western product.[29] In their offices, men were most courteous and professional. No one, including Mayor Tayyip Erdoğan, made me wait. Men also offered tea or coffee. They all shook hands, even though some Islamist men were known not to, and, as a woman, I restrained from initiating the handshake.

I preferred not to use names so that the interviewees could feel more at ease during the interview. All men and some of the women interviewed, particularly public figures such as Sibel Eraslan of the

Refah Party and Nazlı Ilıcak of the Virtue Party, expressed that their interviews could be used with their names. Others agreed that if they remained anonymous, they would feel more comfortable expressing certain issues and we could have more intimate dialogues. With a few exceptions, interviews were taped. They usually lasted about three hours and aimed to explore the political mobilization of Islamist women and think through dichotomies such as private/political, secular/Islamist, and individualist/communalist that had largely defined the parameters within which Islamists were understood. With the small and select group of women leaders interviewed, my aim was not to prove but rather to generate hypotheses which could shed light on both the experiences of these women and the concepts we use to understand Islam, secularism, and politics at large.

In chapter 1, the meaning of women's status in the project of modernity in Turkey is examined so that women's engagement with Islam in the secular Turkish context can be better appreciated. In chapter 2, the Refah Party and the ladies' commissions, their organizational structure, goals, and mobilization strategies in the party are introduced. In chapter 3, women of the ladies' commissions, who they are, how they were attracted to the party, and what kind of satisfaction they got from their work in the party are discussed. Chapter 4 examines the way Refah Party women generate power and mobilize other women for their party. The focus is on what I call "apolitical politicization," the process through which women become politicized in the privacy of their homes and move from the private into the political realm. Significance of local traditions and attributing new functions to traditional modes of social interaction are examined. In chapter 5, the worldviews of these women are examined to show the nature of the boundaries they cross between the secular and Islamist worlds they inhabit. The final chapter, the Conclusion, reconsiders the experience of the Islamist Refah Party women in relation to secularism, liberalism, and democracy.

# Chapter 1

# Women of the Republic and Islam: Between the Private and the Political

This chapter examines the ramifications of being an Islamist woman in Turkey, where women's rights and feminism have a historically unique context. Islamist women of the Refah Party were citizens of a secular state that prided itself on the opportunities it extended to women. Women had long been the most ardent supporters of the Republican regime, because it radically expanded the civil and political rights they could have as citizens. Against this background, the political configuration of the 1980s and the emergence of a feminist oppositionary discourse shaped the political experiences of the Islamist women who were moving into the public space. It is to this context of women and women's rights to which this chapter turns attention.

## SIGNIFICANCE OF WOMEN'S RIGHTS IN THE TURKISH CONTEXT

Women were crucial in the Republican project of modernity. The founding fathers expanded the opportunities women had, because improvement of women's status was intimately linked to the success of the civilizational transformation that was the object of their project of modernity. The project itself was rooted in a radical secularization of the state and society. Islamists opposed to this transformation without much success. The secular 1926 civil code replaced the Islamic legal code and abolished polygamy, unilateral divorce, women's unequal rights in inheritance or custody over children, and unequal opportunities to become witnesses. The new code, with some minor defects, recognized

15

formal male-female equality in society. Thus, improving women's position was a drastic blow to the Islamist opposition. The founding fathers weakened the Islamist opposition at the same time as they improved
women's position through a new secular legal framework.

The minister of justice, who presented the rationale of the draft
bill of the new civil code to Parliament in 1926, primarily argued that
religious law was irreconcilable with the dictates and demands of
contemporary civilization. There was need to discard the religious
code in order to progress and catch up with the new civilization. The
minister argued, "Not to change is a necessity for religions. For this
reason, that religions should remain only matters of conscience is one
of the principles of the civilization of the present century and one of
the most important elements that distinguish the new civilization from
the old. . . . It should not be doubted that our laws that receive their
inspiration from the immutable judgements of religions and still linked
to divine law are the most powerful factor in tying the Turkish nation's
destiny to the stipulations and rules of the Middle Ages, even during
the present century."[1] Unlike other countries, such as Tunisia, that
have expanded civil liberties for men and women within an Islamic
paradigm, the Republican founding fathers argued that religions could
not be changed to accommodate new laws. Instead, and, for many
Islamists ironically, these leaders initiated a far more radical change
regarding what Islam was by redefining its place in communal life.
They restricted the realm in which Islam could have authority, and
they brought in secular laws. Islam was expected to "remain only a
matter of conscience." Expanding women's opportunities and relative
power in relation to men served the goals of secularizing the regime.

To the extent that the new republic did not merely seek to secu-
larize the polity but also to create a national state, expanding women's
status bolstered the efforts to improve nationalist consciousness. In
the Turkish case, invention of tradition to cultivate Turkish nationalism involved harking back to the pre-Islamic and pre-Ottoman Turkic
past in Central Asia. Ziya Gökalp, who provided the ideological underpinnings of Turkish nationalism, fervently argued that women were
considered men's equals in pre-Islamic Turkish past. He elaborated at
length how women could become rulers, commanders, governors, and
ambassadors and how official decrees were cosigned by the "hakan"
(male ruler) and the "hatun" (his wife).[2] Secularization measures, which
expanded opportunities for women, could thus be defended as dictates of national tradition. Reference to national tradition, in turn, legitimized adoption of Western notions of male-female equality to
replace Islamic ones.

Expanding women's rights helped the single-party regime of the new republic to curb its authoritarian image. Kemal Atatürk, who founded the republic and initiated the modernizing reforms, could claim, "Republic means democracy, and recognition of women's rights is a dictate of democracy; hence women's rights will be recognized."[3] He was quite clear about the instrumental nature of expanding women's rights in this case to promote a democratic image. In 1934, women were granted suffrage. İsmet İnönü, who presented the draft bill on suffrage to parliament, explained at length how the Turkish nation prospered and shaped the world when the women of the nation participated in the affairs of the country along with men. In short, expanding women's rights and women's role in the public realm was not merely a symbolic act on the part of the founding fathers but a functional move in promoting the project of modernity.

## LIMITS TO WOMEN'S RIGHTS

Because expansion of women's rights was a dictate of the Republican project of modernity, it was permitted to the extent the founding fathers judged it to be serving the interests of the project. The founding fathers knew the best interests of the nation as well as the best interests of the women. Women's activism, accordingly, was circumscribed by the dictates of an autocratic, westernizing state. There was a tradition, going back to pre-Republican Ottoman regime, of female activists demanding rights for themselves and expressing the struggles of women,[4] but an independent women's movement was not allowed to emerge. When the prominent feminist activist Nezihe Muhittin sought permission in 1923 to establish a party named Women's People's Party, she was denied permission. She was advised to form a women's federation instead. In due time, the federation was closed, because it seemed to be making independent moves, autonomous of the state.[5]

Women were permitted to claim equality with men in the public realm primarily through education and as professionals. Working for the good of the country, many women who could have access to these educational opportunities assumed their new professional roles with a vengeance. They worked in public life to realize the goals of the modernizing state, because expansion of their opportunities was organically linked to the project of modernization. Hamide Topçuoğlu, a vanguard woman of the Kemalist generation, recalled that being a professional "was not 'to earn one's living.' It was to be of use, to fulfill a service, to show success. Atatürk liberated woman by making her responsible."[6] This generation of women believed that they owed their existence to the Kemalist reforms and Kemalism. Their explicit goal was to fight tradition and custom, which were considered to be obstacles in pursuit of the goals of modernization. This intensely emotional allegiance to Atatürk and his reforms had ramifications for contemporary women and their politics. Secular women who were threatened by the Islamist resurgence claimed to be against the Islamists in defense of these reforms.

In their public life, the Kemalist women of the first generation identified themselves with the Turkish "woman" in the singular. In the homogenizing mission of the project of modernity, differences among women were also glossed over. Educated women professionals, mostly women of the middle class, spoke in the name of other women with ease, without regard to differences in ethnicity, religious proclivities, or class.[7] Those women who happened to be different would be integrated into the project of modernity through education and proper exposure to the Kemalist ideals. It was assumed that the expansion of opportunities offered by the Kemalist reforms would allow women to realize all their aspirations.

In private life, patriarchal norms continued to be practiced, perpetuated, and legitimized, despite the formal equality granted under the civil code. Patriarchal norms might not have been eradicated from the public domain, but at least the civil code and women's suffrage undermined the legitimacy given to traditional forms of patriarchal inequality that were practiced in the public realm.[8] In the private domain, however, differences between men and women were rearticulated, and the hierarchic relationship that had traditionally defined male-female relationships reproduced. Even though women were encouraged to be educated and assume professional roles, they were encouraged to play traditional roles as well. After all, women continued to play traditional roles in the West that was emulated. Vocational and technical schools for girls such as Girls Institutes and "evening art schools for girls" (Akşam Kız Sanat Okulları) mobilized women to become good housewives. If women would become housewives under the modernizing Republic, they would have to become modern housewives. Taylorism was adopted in housework, during the early republican era so that women could transform family life in line with the dictates of efficiency, rationality, or westernization.[9] By the second decade of the Republic, about two-thirds of women enrolled in secondary schools were in vocational and technical schools. Housewives continued to constitute the majority of the non-student female population.[10]

Yet, a very significant group of women in the society was educated to become important professional elites. There was a strikingly high percentage of women doctors (even in the 1960s, a quarter of medical school graduates were women) and lawyers (in the seventies in Istanbul, about one-third, and in Turkey about one-fifth of the lawyers were women),[11] a strikingly high number of women (roughly, about one-third) in academic jobs[12] much before the second wave of feminism had its impact in women's education in the West. The Turkish state as well as Turkish men and women prided themselves with how Kemalist reforms emancipated women in Turkey.[13] A tradition of pride with state feminism was invented and institutionalized. Walls were kept between the private and the public realm even though the harem system collapsed and women assumed important positions within the public domain.

There were few women in politics. Even as late as the 1980s, the percentage of women parliamentarians did not surpass the 4.6 percent level of 1935, when women were granted suffrage during the single-party era and when they were practically appointed as representatives on Atatürk's orders. Since the 1960s, Turkey had had a proportional representation system of elections that could better promote women representatives than could majoritarian systems. There were professional women who could potentially be promoted as candidates for parliamentary seats. Female politicians complained that even when structural problems such as economic need and the demands of social roles such as responsibilities of motherhood and marriage were met, it was difficult for women to be nominated as candidates for politically secure parliamentary seats, because men were biased against them.[14] It was only in the 1980s that women took a critical stance when it came to the secular reforms and the project of modernity in the country.

## FEMINISTS AND THE STATE TRADITION

The consensus that was formed in the society regarding state feminism and women's emancipation by the Kemalist reforms was broken in the 1980s. From the early 1980s onwards, a younger generation of educated middle-class professionals who called themselves feminists contested the liberating nature of the reforms.[15] These were the daughters of mostly first-generation, educated professionals whose lives had changed due to the opportunities the Kemalist reforms offered. Unlike their mothers, the daughters could take the opportunities as given and focus on the shortcomings of the system and the instrumental nature of the reforms. In the context of a globalizing world and permeable borders, second-wave feminism began to trickle down. After the 1980 military intervention, the military elite aimed to create a depolitized society in which the right-left cleavages would be obliterated. In this context, women began voicing women's struggles and politicizing women's concerns.[16] Despite the apolitical atmosphere of the 1980s, feminists could voice their issues. The legacy of secular reforms, which altered women's predicament and the legitimacy regarding women's rights discourse in Turkish republican history, facilitated women's endeavors.

Feminists were important in Turkish politics, neither necessarily because of the infrastructural changes they could bring about to improve women's health or education, though they did precipitate significant legal reforms in a legal system that had been untouched since the 1920s, nor because they could politically mobilize the large numbers of women that Islamist women could. Yet, feminists generated a critical discourse that gained legitimacy and influence, if not widespread approval, in the Turkish context. Feminist discourse had its varying impact on Islamist women as well. Important shortcomings of the Republican tradition were analyzed and criticized by these amorphous groups of female activists, novelists, editors, columnists, and media personnel. One of the important criticisms that feminists levied against Republican modernization was regarding the illiberal communitarian nature of the modernizing reforms. Feminists claimed that the instrumental nature of the reforms bridled respect for women's individuality. The leaders and the women of the earlier generation endorsed reforms to the extent that they served communal goals. The new generation demanded respect for their individualism and individual rights, including expression of their sexuality and protection against sexual harassment or domestic violence. The critical engagement of at least some feminists with the modernizing reforms allowed them to support some Islamist women who criticized the confining nature of Turkish secularism.

The younger generation of secular feminists made demands for individualism and individual rights when they voiced the problems they had because they were women. They began from the personal, from what concerned them immediately, to what other women might share in articulating their problems.[17] In this particular process, there was no mission, no explicit goal to save others the way the founding fathers of the Republic had had when they undertook the reforms they did. The feminists confronted the Republican reforms squarely and explicitly discussed not merely how important the reforms concerning women had been for women but rather how important they had been for the project of modernity itself. They explored the conditions in which the reforms were undertaken and argued that the Republican elite reserved the privilege of articulating the best interests of women at the cost of suppressing autonomous feminist initiatives. Contemporary feminists wanted to speak up in their own names and personally articulate the struggles of women, not leave that to men who thought they knew women's interests better than women themselves did. The founding fathers had heralded westernization without liberalism; the contemporary feminists who came up onto the public arena in a context of increasing integration with the West voiced the need for liberal values. Primarily, unlike many of their counterparts of the second-wave feminism in the West, they spoke up in defense of individualism and against communitarian values. In the context of Turkish society, where women were liberated by men who thought they knew women's best interests, feminist demands to speak up in their own voices were refreshing. For secular feminists, individualism did not necessarily mean selfish indulgence in one's pursuit of happiness, as the term connoted in the Turkish cultural context, but rather the ability to speak up in one's own name and express one's own ideas in one's own voice. As such, theirs was a radical cultural and political critique. Issues of domestic violence, sexual harassment in public, sexual repression, and controls over virginity thus surfaced as important items of public agenda.

## ISLAMIST WOMEN

Along with secular feminists, women who had a renewed interest in practicing Islam as they thought it should be practiced challenged the state in Turkey. This broad category of women included self-conscious Muslims who expected the state to respect public expressions of religiosity, some who were ready to fight for these beliefs and others who did not want any confrontation with the state, some who were influenced by feminists and others who rejected them. Their backgrounds varied as well. Although assertion of Islamic identities were most visible among lower and lower-middle-class groups, middle- and upper-middle-class women also sought new identities through Islam. During the past two decades, the high upward mobility within the Islamists circles and the emergence of an Islamist bourgeoisie[18] meant that many Islamist women moved toward the upper classes. Among Islamist women, there were opinion-makers, journalists, professionals, students, and housewives, as well as active members of the Islamist Refah Party. Over time, since the early 1980s when their presence began to be felt, their ideas developed and changed, mostly to become more moderate.[19]

Islamist women, along with Islamist men, presented a radical critique of the Republic. The mere presence of women with their headscarves covering their hair and shoulders in public institutions, particularly universities, was an implicit challenge to Republican attempts to confine religion to the private realm. The more vocal opinion-makers and writers, similar to men, elaborated on how the Republican reforms betrayed Islam and imitated the West, but, unlike most male writers, focused on the predicament of women. Writing in the mid-1980s, Cihan Aktaş, perhaps the most prominent Islamist woman critic, believed that westernization meant adoption of superficial, if not immoral modes of behavior that were accompanied with women's victimization through demeaning, low-paying jobs in the labor market. Aktaş argued that "some privileges granted to some women as rights, could mean injustice to others."[20] She elaborated that the process of westernization gave women the right to go to Europe to follow fashion closely, to snuggle in their furs in winter and wear bikinis in summer. For others, it was the right to become prostitutes and dancers to exhibit their bodies without control. Still others gained the right to work double shifts with meager wages as secretaries, cleaners, and nurses and to come home late at night to do their housework and forego their right to educate their children.[21] Ironically, Aktaş's criticisms are reminiscent of feminist criticisms of capitalist usurpation of women's needs and labor.

Yet, Aktaş, like many other Islamist men and women, did write against "feminism" and "feminists"[22] before she adopted a more mellow and favorable attitude toward feminism. In her earlier writing, feminists conjured up negative images of superficial aping of the West. Feminists, according to Aktaş, included "the psychologically sick, those in search of adventure who run after fantasies, dumb socialites who aspire to give color to their lives, and finally those who consider being a feminist is being enlightened, elite, progressive, and Westernist."[23] Feminists are the "other" to which Aktaş liberally attributes immoral characteristics in order to create a foil against and cultivate the contrasting image of moral Islamist women. Liberation, again according to Aktaş who does not define the term but equates it with feminism, could not make women happy and "satisfy their hunger." Aktaş also insists that feminists could not go beyond a narrow circle, could not reach large masses, and, as a reaction to their imitative culture, could not find a base for themselves. Islam, instead, could bring happiness and reach large numbers of women who were discontented with the imitation of the West. Interestingly, in an interview given to a secular journalist by the end of the 1990s, Aktaş conceded that "feminism was a positive contribution to human history" and that "patriarchy revealed itself whether Islamic or Christian, in all traditions."[24]

Feminist values such as respect for the individual woman, rights of self-determination, and criticism of patriarchal culture had repercussions among women who professed Islam even when they did not want to call themselves feminists.[25] Even though Aktaş was widely read among Islamist women, there were other Islamist women who were less famous but more sympathetic to feminism and feminists as early as the mid-1980s. A group of women writing for the Islamist daily *Zaman* initiated a polemic with the prominent male opinion-makers in the newspaper when they defended secular or radical feminists. The Islamist intellectual Ali Bulaç ridiculed pro-feminist Islamist women with an article entitled "Feminist Women Have Small Brains," which triggered the polemic and ended up with the women having to leave the newspaper.[26]

These women who did not actually call themselves feminists were ready to engage in another polemic, this time not with Islamist men but with radical feminists in the journal *Sosyalist Feminist Kaktüs*. This feminist journal published an article analyzing some of the arguments expressed by the Muslim women in the newspaper *Zaman* that argued for a more egalitarian Islam.[27] The concerned Muslim women responded with a letter to the editor. "A group of Muslim women from Ankara," as they called themselves and signed individually in their letter to *Kaktüs*, argued that the feminists were being elitist and displaying a disparaging attitude, which assumed that they, the secular feminists, and not others, knew the best interests of women. These Muslim women insisted that they saw no contradiction between their religiosity and their refusal to be victimized as women. They argued that whether or not their headscarves imprisoned them to their femininity and procreativity was their own concern.[28] The feminist response denied elitism and drew attention to the significant restrictions that Islam posed on women.[29]

## THE HEADSCARF DEBATE

The different groups of Islamist women—political, apolitical, activist, passivist, professional, student, profeminist, antifeminist—united in their insistence to wear their headscarves, which they declared was a dictate of Islam. The headscarves of the Islamist women were different from those of traditional Turkish women, both in terms of their larger size and in the way they were tied to cover completely the hair as well as the shoulders. The traditional headscarves were smaller in size, and loosely tied with one knot under the chin, which usually allowed hair to show in front.

There were different reasons, different stories, and different interpretations of why women covered. The "rise of Islam," or more specifically, increasing public visibility and influence of Islamist teachings, groups, Quranic schools, sects, and the Refah Party influenced women to cover their heads. Increasing numbers of women in the Prayer Leader and Preacher schools, which grew in strength during the 1980s, and the increasing numbers of women who were accepted to universities, after they finished these schools contributed to the spread of the Islamist headscarves.[30] The orthodox seculars believed and used arguments of how women were manipulated, brainwashed, or paid to cover their heads. Some social scientists argued that the decision to cover one's head according to professed Islamic dictates was a quest for identity or a reaction to the superficial understandings of modernism.[31] Others pointed out that there could be mystical elements, or factors related to social upbringing, in the radical decision to cover one's head.[32]

In response to increasing numbers of covered women in public institutions and universities, the Council of Ministers approved a statute that required female employees and students to dress without head covers.[33] Following this decision, in 1982, the Council of Higher Education banned the use of headscarves in universities. Islamist groups and women with headscarves protested the decision. Under increasing pressure from the Islamists, in 1984, the Council of Higher Education allowed women to cover their hair with a turban, a scarf tied at the back and covering only the hair. The Council deemed turbans as opposed to headscarves to be in line with contemporary dress codes. This time, the secular groups reacted. Ex-Chief of Staff, then-President Kenan Evren took the initiative to ban the turban and, in early 1987, the Council withdrew the article allowing the turbans. The students were, once again, expected to dress according to contemporary dress codes (which meant Western dress codes). The decision was again relaxed in the spring of the same year in a meeting of the university rectors. In 1989, the Council of Higher Education reversed its previous stance and withdrew the article which prohibited the use of turbans indoors in the universities.

Politicians and the judiciary also joined the controversy, with their own internal cleavages over the issue. The Social Democrats that claimed the heritage of Republican secularism were against headcovering. The center right parties were inclined to ignore the issue and let women dress as they would. In 1987, Prime Minister Turgut Özal of the center right Motherland Party tried to pass a law to relax the dress code in the universities. President Evren vetoed the initiative.

The judiciary declared headcovering in the universities unlawful. Some decisions given by lower courts were favorable to those who were for headcovering, but the higher courts of the Council of State and the Constitutional Court rejected these verdicts. In 1984, the Council of State rejected an appeal to withdraw the 1982 statute of the Council of Higher Education that banned headcovering. In 1987, the Council of State again rejected a similar court case. In 1989, the Constitutional Court decided that the statute of the Council of Higher Education allowing the use of the turban in the universities was unconstitutional and annulled it.

The issue was carried to the European Human Rights Commission as well. When a university administration refused to prepare the diplomas of two graduating students who insisted that their pictures with headcovers be used in their diplomas, the students sued the latter and eventually took the case to the European Human Rights Commission. The Commission rejected the case as well.

With their protests against the ban, the Islamist women did not merely criticize Republican secularism but, in a widespread act of civil disobedience, presented a radical challenge to state authority. The protest was costly both for the state, which had difficulty enforcing its decisions, as well as the many women involved who had to abandon ambitions for professional careers and even plans to complete their university education. By the 1990s, women who were subject to overt state intervention in attending universities and being employed in state institutions with their heads covered began narrating their stories of victimization. They wrote books and novels about the injustices perpetrated against women with head covers.[34] By the end of the 1990s, organizations such as Özgür-Der and Ak-Der were established to defend the rights of the Islamist women against the regulations of the state, which prohibited headcovering.

## The Case for Headscarves

Women who demanded to be admitted to universities with headscarves argued that it was their basic civil liberty. They referred to Article 24 of the 1982 Constitution, which guarantees freedom of religious expression, and Article 10, which prohibits discrimination before law due to religious belief and differences in language, ethnicity, gender. They insisted on their right to education protected by Article 42 of the Constitution.

Women with headscarves who were not admitted to universities were discriminated against not merely because of religious belief, but also because they are women. Men who shared the same beliefs with women and thought that women's headcovering was a dictate of religion were admitted to universities; their heads were uncovered.

The women who covered their heads had a different reading of Islam than the state was willing to accommodate. They believed that, according to Islam, women have to be covered at all times in public spaces. Ironically, the Directorate of Religious Affairs under the Prime Minister did not ever publicly refute the Islamic dictate that women cover in public. However, the statist understanding of Islam assumed that Muslim women could be uncovered in the public domain and still be good Muslims. The Islamist women were ready to protest, in defense of their understanding of Islam, in opposition to what was enforced on them. They could be seen as perforating the boundaries of the narrowly defined freedom of action for religious individuals.

*The Case for the Ban*

The higher courts gave the most decisive arguments against the headscarf. In response to the argument for the headscarf as a dictate of political liberalism, the courts argued that it would obstruct the latter. The courts and those opposed to the ban made various arguments.[35] One argument that was frequently used was that headcovering restricted women's liberties: The Council of State explicitly argued that headcovering was opposed to women's liberation. Many others, including some but not all feminists, opposed the headscarf, because they saw it as a means of controlling women. Among secular groups, the headscarf had long been associated with limiting women's options in self expression and with Islamic law where women are deemed to have unequal rights to men regarding marriage, inheritance, and divorce (because Islamic law allows for polygamy, unilateral divorce, and a greater share of inheritance to men).

Another important argument focused on headcovering as a symbol of opposition to the Republic, namely, secularism. The Council of State argued that "rather than an innocent custom, it (the headscarf) has become a symbol of a worldview opposed to the fundamental principles of the Republic."[36] The Constitutional Court explained that it was a symbol opposed to secularism and defended the statist conception of secularism: "In a laicist order, religion is prevented from politicization and becoming an administrative device and kept in its real respectable place in people's consciences."[37] Headscarves, thus it was deduced, could not be recognized within the limits of religious freedom (Article 24 of the Constitution).

It was further argued that headcovering would lead to unequal treatment among students. The constitutional court argued that allowing the headcover would not only be a privilege given to Islamist students but it would generate the circumstances for their unequal treatment by differentiating them from others. Contrary to the claims of the Islamists, the court argued that the headscarf was against the principle of equal treatment before law (Article 10 of the 1982 Constitution). The argument was similar to those used in France where religious differences were expected to be neutralized in public schools.[38] When the headscarf issue was taken to the European Human Rights Commission, the commission acknowledged the right of a secular state to restrict religious practices and maintained that this restriction would allow students of different beliefs to coexist. It was further argued that "particularly in countries where the vast majority of the population belong to a particular religion, exhibition of the rituals and symbols of this religion without regard to any restrictions of place and form can cause pressure on students who do not practice this religion or instead belong to an other religion."[39]

Finally, it was argued that headcovering insinuated the threat of organizing the state according to the dictates of Islam. The principle of religious freedom, as stated in the Constitution, explicitly precluded organizing state's social, economic, political, or legal order, even partially, according to religious dictates. Instituting the dress code according to religious dictates would be in contradiction with this requirement. Thus, the state aimed to draw its "boundaries of freedom of action vis-à-vis religious dictates" outside the domain of headscarves, to protect itself from encroachment of Islamic law.

The headscarf debate was a complicated issue involving at times simplistic, even essentialist, assumptions on both sides. It was at the heart of Islamist politics in Turkey. After the Refah Party was closed, the support Fazilet Party members gave to legitimize headscarves precipitated the closing of the party and the banning of two of its female members from politics.[40] After the Adalet ve Kalkınma Party came to power, a number of headscarf crises took place, though the government contained them. While the struggle between Islamist women with headscarves and the state continues, it was the context in which the Refah Party attracted Muslim women into its ranks in the early 1990s.

## FEMINISTS AND ISLAMISTS

The Islamist challenge to the republic had its repercussions. Within the secular feminist ranks, demands evolved over time, particularly in response to Islamist groups. An older group of women who called themselves Kemalist feminists began to organize in the late 1980s in response to what they perceived as the Islamist threat in society. They were concerned that the rising tide of Islamism would undermine women's rights that had been secured by Kemalist reforms. They argued that Islam restricted women's rights: It allowed polygamy, unilateral divorce by men, unequal share of inheritance for women, if not other restrictions. Politicized Islam could threaten the secular legal framework, including the civil code, which insured that restrictions of the Islamic code became irrelevant for women in Turkey.

Rather than issues of sexual harassment or sexual repression, the Kemalist feminists prioritized fighting illiteracy and expanding the secular educational opportunities for women that the Republican reforms had initiated. They argued that increasing literacy would undermine the appeal of Islam. Unlike the more radical feminists, and ironically more similar to Islamists, the Kemalist feminists felt comfortable with the communitarian as opposed to individualistic values in society. As was an earlier generation, they were imbued with fervor to uphold the reforms. As one of their prominent members put it: "If we could rid ourselves of that individualism, I wonder if we have the right to be individual feminists?"[41] Even when there was tolerance for individualism, it was endorsed with skepticism and with a condition.

Kemalist feminists believed that Islamist women had been misguided and needed help. The same feminist who was skeptical of individualistic feminism explained as such, "I do not believe it is her free choice [to cover her head]. I am angry with those who have captured her brains. The way they have put her forward like a flag without showing and offering her options and manipulating some material interests, this has caused me grief."[42] When they were organized to establish a foundation (Çağdaş Yaşamı Destekleme Derneği—Association to Promote Contemporary Life), the president of the organization explained their engagement as follows:

> For some time now, we have been confronted by a serious and surreptitious reactionary movement that hides behind the curtain of "woman to dress as she wishes" but in reality struggles to return our society to the darkness of the Middle Ages. We do not doubt that this reactionary movement, led by a handful of dogmatic diehard Islamists who have roots outside [the country] and who deceive many of our well-meaning, innocent people, sees the destruction of the secular republic as its first goal and pursues the establishment of a Shariat order. We came together with the awareness of

this danger and the authority that Atatürk's reforms have given us in order to protect the Atatürk reforms, the secular republic and our rights which are an inalienable part of these [reforms and the secular republic].[43]

Other feminists, particularly among the younger generation, were not as intimidated by the Islamists nor did they all argue that Islamist women covered because they were brainwashed. They felt that questioning women's decision to cover their heads would be analogous to questioning their agency. After all, women had historically been denied access to many opportunities, because their ability to make choices was questioned.[44] They knew that their main enemy was sexism, and sexism existed in Islam as well. They thus could see a common denominator of solidarity with Islamist women. The radical feminists who gathered around the journal *Pazartesi* explicitly supported Islamist women who were fighting for the permission to attend universities with their heads covered. When the secular constituency of the journal reacted to the support given to Islamist women, *Pazartesi* did not back down. To the contrary, editorials were issued in defense of the journal's position and on why it supported Islamist women. The editorials criticized the Kemalist understanding of secularism, which prohibited Islamist women from attending universities with their headscarves, and argued that their understanding of feminism was critical of the Kemalist discourse on women, which decided what was in the best interest of women rather than allowing women to decide for themselves.[45] They argued that "to fight political Islam as women, they had to expose its sexism, contest the sexist undertakings of the Refah Party government without concession, explain how the Shariat was against women, rather than house-arresting women who covered their heads."[46]

Expansion of women's rights had defined the parameters within which the Republic chose to assert its newly acquired autonomy and priorities. The secular identity of the Republic was organically linked to the question of women's rights. By the 1980s when the Republican project was critically reviewed, Islamist women, along with secular feminists, were important contributors to this critical enterprise. They defined themselves in opposition to as well as in relation to the secular modernization project and its secular feminist critics. They were products of the history that they explicitly rejected. Islamist women shaped their identity within this unique configuration of politics. It was under these conditions that the Refah Party Ladies' Commissions organized and recruited Islamist women into its ranks.

# Chapter 2

# Refah Party and the Organization of The Ladies' Commissions

If the broader context in which Islamist women defined themselves was the Republican project of modernity, its secularism and its critical feminism, the more immediate context in which they worked was the Islamist Refah Party. The particular orientation of the party defined Islamist women's political rhetoric. The party organization shaped the contours of their mobilizational activity. To understand the political framework in which Islamist women worked as members of the Refah Party Ladies' Commissions, we have to examine the party itself. Refah was an important locus of Islamist politics in Turkey. As a powerful actor in the institutionalized political structure of the country, the party channeled people's needs at the same time as it cultivated them to consolidate its power and ideology.[1] The appeal of the party was intimately tied to the appeal of political Islam.

There have been various explanations, some related to political culture and others to political economy, for the rise of Islamist politics in the country. Şerif Mardin argued that Islam always had an appeal in the context of Republican Turkey, because the Republican ideology had been unable to appeal to the hearts of the population with its pragmatic, positivist, rationalist ideology: "superficiality and lack of organic linkages with society, of Kemalism"[2] allowed the Islamists to fill the vacuum created in the lives of the people. Islam had an appeal that the statist ideology of the Republic could not have. This powerful explanation led to further elaborations about the important role of the state in controlling religion[3] or accommodating it,[4] which precipitated Islamist reaction. Analysts drew attention to the deep-rooted cultural

31

confrontation between the Islamist and Kemalist lifestyles, which defined the dynamics of Islamist ascendance[5] and pointed to the crises
of national identity in the context of global modernity that instigated
an Islamic backlash.[6]

Other explanations for the rise of political Islam pointed to the
importance of political economy. Internal migration from rural to urban areas, which had continued since the 1950s and accelerated over
time, was seen as a significant cause.[7] The newly migrant population
of the metropolitan areas had difficulties in adapting to the economic
and cultural demands of urban life. Pressures to create employment
and integrate the newcomers to the urban environment mounted. The
Islamist call responded to these demands and appealed to the norms
and values of migrants' rural background. Others drew attention to
external factors and to the process of globalization of the world
economy. Globalization had its consequences: It destabilized the world
order and allowed for the economic deprivation of many while it
expanded the opportunities of the few.[8] As the country became part of
this world order with its pro-Western ideology, it allowed for the
economic deprivation of lower and lower-middle classes.

In this context of political, cultural, and economic processes favorable to the strengthening of political Islam, the Refah Party, which
was founded in 1983, increased its appeal to large sectors of the population. In the 1987 general elections, the party received 7.2 percent of
the votes. In the 1991 elections, doubtful that they could surmount the
10 percent threshold, which could keep them from sending delegates
to the parliament, the party leaders made an alliance with the nationalist Milliyetçi Hareket (National Action) Party. The alliance was able
to get 16.2 percent of the votes. The upward trend of the Refah Party
was sealed with the 1994 local elections, when it received 19.7 percent
of the vote and won the elections in large cities, including Istanbul
and Ankara. In the 1995 elections, the party came out as the largest
one in the country, with 21.4 percent of the vote.

How did the party appeal to this increasing portion of the electorate? The party program stated the main goal of the party to be "the
public construction and development of the country" coupled with "
its cultural and moral development." These goals would be carried
out with "national characteristics and specificities" in mind.[9] Even
though this general description did not specify what "the national
characteristics and specificities of the country" were or in what direc-
tion "the cultural and moral development of the country" would take
place, the party forcefully underlined the importance of religion and
Islam both in the party program and thereafter. It espoused the ide-

ology of so-called National Outlook (Milli Görüş), inherited from its pre-1980 predecessor the Milli Selamet Party. The National Outlook represented, it was argued an "authentic," historically anchored, nationalist perspective to solve the problems the country faced due to rampant modernization and imitation of the West.[10] The National Outlook criticized the West and traced many of the country's problems to Turkey's project of Westernization.

The party pursued its National Outlook by cultivating a dichotomous worldview. There was the Refah Party and, opposed to it, the "parties of imitation," which included all its rivals. The Refah Party defined itself in relation to these parties of imitation. The parties of imitation, according to this view, which was elaborated through the party electoral declarations and the speeches of its leaders, upheld "power," whereas the Refah Party upheld "justice." The former aimed to be "a satellite of the West and change the history of the nation," and the Refah Party aimed for "autonomy and reclaiming their honorable place in history." The former aimed to "obliterate the identity of the nation," and the Refah Party aimed to "initiate a new world and make Turkey the leader of this new world."[11]

The diachronic depictions were embellished in relation to the economic realm. According to the proponents of the Refah Party, the parties of imitation sought to be part of a system of exploitation characterized by a capitalism based on destructive interest rates, whereas they sought a "just economic order." The former were characterized by the presence of the International Monetary Fund, exploitative interest rates, taxes, windfall profits, and waste, whereas they promoted a nationalist worldview (i.e., a religious one), mobilization for increased productivity, removal of obstacles on the way to production, fair sharing of what is produced, and prevention of waste.

On the political domain, "the parties of imitation," according to the Refah Party worldview, aimed to maintain a state that was a "prison guard" characterized by pressure; confrontation with the people, its beliefs (i.e., religion), and history; and an administration that was like an empty shell. The Refah Party, in contrast, aimed to promote a state that served its people, "a waiter state" respectful of human rights and liberties, that was the representation of people's beliefs and history and a union of the state and the nation. The cadres that these parties had were also depicted through a binary opposition. The parties of imitation did not have cadres with moral powers; neither did they have the will, the initiative, or the ability to serve for love of worship, nor did they have any plans. The Refah Party had virtuous cadres with conviction, will, ability to take initiative and to serve for the love of worship. The party, in short, had conviction, science, a plan, cadres, and the ability to pursue and bring its goal to conclusion.[12]

This didactic, parsimonious worldview was the main discursive tool with which the Refah Party reached the electorate. Its advocates elaborated this dichotomy in their interactions with their prospective constituencies. For example, on the issue of morality, they detailed the immoral community their rivals brought about. This moral destruction was partly precipitated by television programs that showed immoral foreign films and advertised drinking and fornication. The print media propagated promiscuity with colorful, indecent photographs that they published and poisoned the youth. Beaches were filled with nudes. To continue the destruction of public morality, millions of dollars were loaned from abroad under the pretext of encouraging touristic investments. Millions of dollars were paid to buy gambling machines to corrupt morals. Bribery and undeserved profits reigned.[13]

In place of this, the Refah Party promised "a just spiritual and moral order." In this new order, spirituality, not materialism, would reign. Youths as well as ordinary citizens would be given opportunities for religious, spiritual, and moral education. The ordinary citizen would have an opportunity to find out what his religion taught.[14] Mosques and Quranic schools would be opened to fulfill the citizens' religious needs. Prayer Leader and Preacher schools would be founded.

On the economic front, the party came up with the vague concept of a "just economic order" that it promised its constituency. The just economic order was realized when banking with interest was abolished. According to the Refah worldview, interest was the cause of capitalist exploitation. Because of interest banking, those with money increased what they already had, enriching the minority and impoverishing the majority.[15] The party would abolish interest as well as all taxes except those from its own production. The taxes gathered under the previous system were siphoned off to pay interest-accruing debts to foreign banks, support businessmen who received credits because of fictive exports, and subsidize government extravaganzas. The party would stop the printing of money, which fueled inflation. Instead it would initiate heavy industry, which would secure the economic independence of the country and create employment for the unemployed.

During the early 1990s when Kurdish separatism and Kurdistan Workers' Party, Partiya Karkeren Kurdistan (PKK) terrorism was high on the agenda of the population, the Refah Party addressed this tough issue through an appeal to Islamic solidarity. Religion, which Republican secularism aimed to privatize, was now used as a tool for trespassing ethnic cleavages, in the name of nationalist/religious solidarity and votes from the Kurdish regions, particularly in Eastern and South Eastern Anatolia. The party was an articulate critic of the militarist solution that the governments in power sought to the Kurdish problem. The Refah Party took a radical stand and accused the Turkish state for materialist and racist policies that they followed in the region.[16] The Eastern and Southeastern regions where the Kurdish population lived were economically ignored and politically violated. The state neither generated projects to develop the region nor allowed the Kurds to use their mother tongues in their media and schooling.

The Refah Party argued that Kurds were the Muslim brothers who had to be given their political and economic rights. Throughout history they had lived as Muslim brothers and defended this soil against the enemy under the Ottoman Caliph, their religious leader. The party promised to uplift the embargo on Iraqi products, which undermined the economy of the region even further, and prepare a special development program to strengthen Eastern and Southeastern Turkey. They promised to solve the problem of terrorism with more appropriate, modern technology and educate professional teams to fight in the mountains. They would allow for freedoms to be recognized and thus prepare the conditions where Muslims could live as brothers.[17]

The party promoted its National Outlook and calls for Muslim brotherhood not merely within the confines of the nation-state but also outside its borders. The present regime and the "parties of imitation" all continued to ally themselves to the colonizing West, which did not want to accept Turkey within Western borders. The present regime insisted on becoming part of the European Union, which did not even want Turkey. Meanwhile, the Refah Party argued that Turkey's place was not the Christian (i.e., European) union based on the Treaty of Rome established on the advice of Pope Pio the XII, but rather the union of the Muslim countries of the world.[18] The leader of the party, Erbakan, argued that the Refah Party would ensure the highest degree of collaboration amongst Muslim countries and groups in the world. To reach this goal, a "United Nations of Muslim Countries" would be established to counter the United Nations in which no Muslim country had a right to veto. An "Organization of Muslim Countries Defense Cooperation" would effectively counter NATO to prevent unfair assaults on Muslim countries and help to promote justice. A "Muslim Countries Common Market" would facilitate economic cooperation within the Islamic world. Over time, there would be movement toward a "Muslim Countries Common Monetary Unit." Finally, an "Organization of Muslim Countries Cultural Cooperation" would coordinate the scientific, technological, and art ventures amongst Muslim countries.[19] In all these initiatives, Turkey would assume a leadership role amongst Muslim countries that it had lost with the disintegration of the Ottoman Empire and the banishment of the Ottoman Caliph.

Within this world-view and the ideology of National Outlook, women had a curious position. They were the pillars of the moral order that the party propagated, yet, as women per se, they were readily ignored. The religiously inspired moral order depended on women both for its establishment and its success. Women were expected to be proper wives and mothers who would socialize their children to be the moral men and women constituting the religious community. On the other hand, the success of this moral order depended on women's restraint, or, depending on how one looked at it, women expressing themselves, their sexuality, and their material needs in a religiously proscribed correct way. If the West was given to prostitution, drugs, profanity and consumerism, it was primarily women who would have to teach their children to despise this Western culture. Again, it was women who would practice what they taught. Thus, the men who earned the money would not be wasting it on consumerism, and there would not be prostitutes available, only "decent" women who covered up so as not to tempt men.

The program of the Refah Party, just like its predecessor the Milli Selamet Party, had no reference to women. Like the Milli Selamet Party before it, the Refah Party included a discussion of the family in its program without any reference to women.[20] After all, it was in the context of the family, not as individual women, that women could fulfill the critical role they were expected to fulfill within this religious worldview. In other party documents, concerns for the future of the family and deterioration of family life or divorce rates came up; family was duly singled out as the pillar of society on which social development would be based.[21] In the declaration prepared for the 1991 general elections, there was a section named "Ladies, Mothers" which elaborated the role the party expected women to play in the society:

> In society, ladies and mothers are given important duties. According to our beliefs, 'Heaven is under the feet of mothers.' In the tradition of our nation ladies and mothers have always deserved respect and affection. Let us never forget

that Sultan Alpaslans, Sultan Osmans, Sultan Fatihs and great scholars like Akşemseddin people who have been examples of morality and virtue have been raised by their mothers. Mothers of today and tomorrow will raise those who will build and serve the great Turkey once again. What a great goal, what an honorable service!"[22]

Because maternal roles were such a priority, the party promised ladies and mothers services that would allow these roles to be assumed with ease. Marriage would be facilitated, and for those who wanted to marry, interest-free marriage credits would be given. For those ladies who wanted, opportunities would be given for either full-day or half-day employment outside the house that would not undermine their responsibilities and duties within the family.

"Woman," in the singular, and this time not "ladies" or "mothers," would play an active role in the foundation of the "Just Order" and would found the new world with her man. This claim was a public recognition and legitimization of the role women would play in the party ranks. "Woman–man conflict," it was declared in the same article, is a fruit of the conflictual worldview based on power. From the perspective of the National Outlook, not conflict but cooperation and solidarity is fundamental between man and woman. The party thus recognized the complementarity of women to men as opposed to their equality, a stance that underlined the crude essentialist arguments about women's difference from, rather than equality to, men. "Woman," within this Nationalist Outlook, would not be exploited, and she would not be allowed to be used as a tool for advertisement or commerce. This promise was also consistent with the anti-Western worldview that the party aimed to propagate.

The party successfully appealed to a large group of Muslim women on the headscarf issue. Ironically, the support the party gave to women who wanted to legitimize wearing of headscarves in universities and public institutions was not expressed as a women's issue per se. The issue of the headscarf came up in discussions of the authoritarian nature of the state and the need for democratization. "Headscarf oppression," as it was called, was part of freedom of religious expression almost independent of women.[23] However, party officials and advocates always made it unequivocally clear that they supported women's right to wear their headscarves in universities and as public employees and promised that women would be given this right when they came to power. For many women, the promise had strong appeal and was a serious reason to support the party.

## THE REFAH PARTY CONSTITUENCY

The Refah Party successfully expanded the coalition of interests that had supported its predecessor the Milli Selamet Party and appealed to a broad constituency.[24] It has been claimed that the Milli Selamet Party primarily received votes from small provincial businessmen, artisans, and conservative populations of the provincial areas.[25] The Refah Party built on this core to include working classes in large urban cities, mostly new immigrants. This important success meant the transfer of votes from urban lower- and lower-middle-class voters from the social democratic to the Refah Party. The social democrats, who were entrapped in statist secularism of the Republic and fear of Islamic fundamentalism, could not develop an alternative critical discourse to the one put forth by the Refah Party. The latter's criticism of the capitalist system and exploitation of the poor by the rich, coupled with an appeal to the primordial norms and culture that the migrants brought with them to the urban areas, were important in consolidating the new coalition of interests the Refah Party built.

A crucial group in this new coalition was the emerging class of Muslim businessmen and professionals. The party developed organic ties with the Muslim capitalists who benefited from the pro-Islamic environment and contacts they could cultivate in this context to increase their strengths. Islamic networks began to open up channels of upward mobility to their members.[26] In 1990, pro-Islamic businessmen founded their own voluntary association, MUSIAD, The Association of Independent Industrialists and Businessmen, as a rival to the large mostly Istanbul-based TUSIAD, The Association of Turkish Industrialists and Businessmen.[27] Members of MUSIAD resented the organic ties big business traditionally had to the state and they were willing to seek alternative ties of political collaboration. They had long been the marginal business groups in the Chambers of Commerce and Industry, the traditional corporatist organization of business in the country.

Along with this enlarged coalition, which primarily centered on economic interests, was the Kurdish constituency, which the Refah Party could appeal to with its comparatively liberal discourse on this issue. In the 1991 general elections, the Refah Party could get 16.6 percent of the votes in the Kurdish-populated Eastern and Southeastern provinces of the country; the figure rose to 27.3 percent in the 1994 local elections and to 27.2 percent in the 1995 general elections.[28]

## THE REFAH PARTY AND DEMOCRACY

The Refah Party generated controversy regarding its commitment and contributions to democracy in the country. The party was closed by a Constitutional Court decision when the court ruled that it had become a locus of anti-secular activity. Even though the nature and limits of Turkish secularism was disputed, to the extent that secularism was necessary for democracy, for many, the decision of the Constitutional Court was enough proof that the party was a threat to democracy.

Party members, including its prominent leaders, sent dubious messages to their constituency regarding their commitment to democracy. Erbakan became notorious for his verbal blunder in the parliament when he said that they would come to power anyway "with blood or without blood." He was also quoted to have claimed in a party convention that the party soon would have so many members that elections would no longer be necessary.[29] When Tayyip Erdoğan was head of the Istanbul Refah Party organization, he was quoted as saying, "Democracy is a means, and not an end" for their party.[30]

These flagrantly antidemocratic statements made by the party leaders were accompanied by their illiberal practices guided by short-term interests.[31] The party that preached Muslim solidarity with the Kurdish population of the country and argued that Kurdish ethnic identity be recognized nevertheless voted to have the immunities of the pro-Kurdish Democracy Party (DEP) parliamentarians removed when the parliamentarians of the Democracy Party were accused of separatist propaganda in 1994. The party exhibited an illiberal attitude not merely toward the Kurds but also towards the West, Kemalists, Zionists, and even Africans through condescending speech if not overt action.[32] The traditional division of labor that the party propagated could also be considered an illiberal stance that could obstruct women's opportunities for self-fulfillment outside the home.

Yet, the Refah Party, as an establishment that could appeal to the interests of the marginal groups in society and in the peripheral regions of the rural as well as urban areas, expanded the scope of political participation in the democratic process.[33] These large groups of voters could have their needs and voices heard through the Refah Party, which played an important oppositional role if not an effective leadership role. The Refah Party thus extended the spectrum of mainstream politics. It provided an opportunity for upward mobility; new elites emerged and vitalized politics.[34]

The Refah Party insisted on the importance of freedom of con-science and religious belief. Even though this insistence was mainly a pragmatic and not a particularly principled one, geared to promoting the party's own worldview, nevertheless, it was a significant chal-lenge to the establishment ideology, particularly its interpretation of secularism. While the party might not have been able to change the restrictive definition of Republican secularism, which aimed to control religion not merely disassociate it from political life, it challenged a taboo by questioning the appropriateness of this particular understand-ing of secularism. The Republic itself, its nationalist communalism, and the limited recognition of individual rights were thus opened to debate. To the extent that this challenge highlighted the limits of the liberal tradition in the country, it was a contribution to freedom of thought and broader democratic participation. The role of women, priority given to traditional roles, and the headscarf controversy de-fined the parameters of this challenge. It was within this context that women organized within the party.

## EVOLUTION OF THE LADIES COMMISSIONS

Within the Refah Party, the need to consider women as a support group began to be felt after the 1987 elections. Perhaps the earliest and most vocal advocate of the idea of organizing women within the party orga-nization and trying to reach other women was Tayyip Erdoğan, at the time head of the Refah Party Istanbul organization. The project was adopted, but not without opposition. The more conservative within the party argued that women's place was the home and that it was inappro-priate to expect women to work within the party ranks. Besides, if the party could reach enough men, women would vote along with their men. Those who proposed recruiting women to the party believed that women could help with recruiting men as well as other women. The opposition was contained, and in 1989 women close to the Refah Party circles, friends and relatives of the men in the administrative organs of the party, began to be educated to form the women's commissions. Tayyip Erdoğan personally trained the first group of women, who would form the first commissions. Those who continued to be displeased in-sisted that in his seminars, Erdoğan should preserve Islamic modesty and turn his back to the headscarved ladies in the room.

The *1990 Work Schedule of the Refah Party Istanbul Organization* (Refah Partisi İstanbul İl Teşkilatı 1990 Yılı Çalışma Programı) explic-itly and very urgently called attention to the need to increase the activities of the party toward women. In a section called "Deficiencies," which was placed right after the Introduction, it was stated: "The inadequacy of our work related to ladies is acknowledged by all members of our organization, and among those issues that need to be addressed and solved urgently, it ranks first."[35] The Refah Party leaders recognized that in order to grow they had to go beyond the constituency that the Milli Selamet Party bequeathed to them. Even though the Milli Selamet Party had played a key role in the politics of the 1970s in Turkey, it never received more than 11 percent of the votes, even in its strongest days. The leaders of the Refah Party had broader horizons and aimed to build a mass party with a large following. For this purpose, they were ready to challenge taboos. Allowing women to participate in party politics was one such taboo that needed to be contested. The immediate family members, mostly housewives, formed the niche with which the party began mobilizing women and expanding its supporters.

*Organization of the Ladies' Commissions*

The Refah Party had a wide organizational web throughout the country.[36] The party was organized hierarchically at the regional, provincial, district, and neighborhood levels. At the neighborhood level the party assigned representatives for each street to collect information about the people living in the area and to offer needed services. The party organization was sensitive to local needs and problems and took care to adopt the official party lines to local needs. The ladies' commissions became part of this widespread, efficient, and effective organization.

Because the 1981 Constitution prohibited the parties from organizing women's branches, women's organization within the party was carried out as a commission activity under the supervision of the party's public relations branch. The name of the commission was peculiar, drawing attention to a difference that the party and the commission had from others. It was called "ladies' " rather than "women's." In Republican history, no political or social association was named "ladies' " instead of "women's" association or organization. The former conjured up a traditional form of deference that upheld women bound by restrictive communal norms. It was a form of reference used more in private relationships, usually in singular, together with the first name of the woman in question. The use of the plural 'ladies' to qualify a public organization harked back to pre-Republican times when the word was more commonly used.

Even though there were women who did not like the name "ladies' " and did not understand why the commissions were called 'ladies" and not, 'women's' commissions, an interviewee approvingly narrated to us the explanation of a male party official: not all women could become ladies, however, the Refah Party believed that all women were actually ladies. The preference for the word 'ladies' rather than 'women' reflected the high esteem in which the party held women. The euphemism also revealed that the male leaders who named the organization considered that the word 'woman' needed to be substituted by a more graceful or 'polite' alternative. Women were not acceptable as such; they had to be something else, preferably ladies.

Those who objected to the word pointed that there was a divisive, class bias associated with the word 'hanımlar' ('ladies'), as opposed to 'women,' which was more encompassing. These responses reflected the respect for lower-class sensibilities that those in critical positions within the ladies' commissions had. The commissions had been most active and most successful among lower- and lower-middle-class women in metropolitan areas. The active members of the commissions were thus sensitive to the exclusionary nature of the term. To the extent that not all women in actual life were ladies, or at least were not or did not want to be called ladies because being called a lady meant you had to conform to certain socially acceptable norms and values, the commissions reflected the conservative bias the party had toward women.

In theory, the ladies' commission was one of the several commissions tied to the public relations branch of the party. The number of commissions the provincial organization had depended on the province. For example, in the Ankara Provincial Organization of the party, the ladies' commission was one of seven.[37] The other six were the youth commission, professional associations commission, workers' commission, civil servants' commission, retired people's commission, and handicapped persons' commission. In Istanbul, it was one of eleven, which also included the local administration, education, research, human rights, environment, and health commissions, besides those Ankara had.[38] Even though formally the ladies' commission seemed to be one of several—some of them quite insignificant—commissions, in reality it had a unique position within the party establishment with an organization parallel to that of the central party organs. Its goals and mission within the party structure were no less important.

The goals of the ladies' commissions within the provinces included the following:

  a. ensuring the institutionalization and effectiveness of the ladies' commissions at provincial-level and district-level organizations.

b. organizing "enlarged monthly consultative meetings," with the participation of the provincial-level and district-level "ladies' commissions."

c. organizing seminars, conferences, panels, symposiums, and the like concerning ladies' problems at the provincial or district levels.

d. preparing propositions that present the party's National Outlook solutions concerning ladies' problems.

e. ensuring the increase in ladies' membership.

f. organizing fairs, plays, and fashion shows directed toward ladies.

g. ensuring the participation of women with oratory powers in the propaganda work of the party.[39]

Ladies' commissions were vertically organized and horizontally tied to the central organs of the party. In Ankara, the President's Office of the Refah Party Ladies' Commission 'RP Hanımlar Komisyonu Genel Başkanlığı,' was the organizational center of the commission. Below the office of the president were the ladies' commissions organized at the province level, 'İl teşkilatları,' which were loosely overseen by regional supervisors, 'bölge teşkilatları.' Under the provincial-level organizations were the district organizations, 'ilçe teşkilatları.' Under the district organizations were at times the administratively larger 'belde,' or county organizations, and in most places the smaller 'mahalle' or quarter, organizations, and under them were the 'sandık' or ballot box, organizations. At every organizational level, the ladies' commissions were horizontally tied to the relevant central party organization.[40] At every province and district level of the main organization, a male member of the party represented the ladies' commission at the administrative council. Members of the ladies' commissions at the provinces and presidents of the ladies' commissions at the district organizations were invited to attend the monthly enlarged council meetings ('divan') of the corresponding central party organization.[41] The ladies' commissions were hierarchically lower in status than the central party administration at the same organizational level and could be present only in designated meetings of the central party organization.

Even though lower in rank, the organizational structure of the ladies' commission paralleled that of the central party organization. Commissions in provinces with larger urban areas designated as metropolitan centers, such as Istanbul and Ankara, had twenty-five members and twenty-five auxiliary members, constituting a total of 50 members, including the president and the vice president.[42] These twenty-five members and their auxiliaries were responsible for twenty-five different units:[43]

1. presidency
2. organization
3. electoral work
4. propaganda
5. public relations
6. local administration coordination
7. foreign relations
8. economic and social issues
9. secretariat
10. accountant
11. financial issues
12. education
13. orators
14. youth
15. professional associations
16. personnel
17. manager
18. information processing
19. planning and research
20. press and publications
21. professional chambers
22. trade unions
23. nongovernmental organizations
24. social and cultural activities
25. documentation and archives.

These fifty members constituted the administrative council, 'yönetim kurulu,' which met every week to discuss their plan of action, program the activities of the commission, and evaluate what was done.

A group of nine from this council was the executive council, or 'icra kurulu,' which was responsible not merely for running the daily or hourly planned activities of the commission but also steering the course of action which would be taken in the administrative council meetings. Members of the executive council included the president of the provincial organization and those responsible from these units: organization, electoral works, propaganda, public relations, local administration, secretariat, economic and social issues, education, and youth. The executive council met weekly as well. In smaller provinces, the commissions and the administrative councils included thirty members, seven of whom constituted the executive council.

At the district level, where the population was less than 50,000, the ladies commissions had fifteen members. In districts of metropolitan provinces with a population of more than 50,000, fifteen members and fifteen auxiliary members, that is, a total of thirty members constituted the ladies' commissions.[44] Similar to the provincial organization, the administrative councils of the district organizations included all their members, whereas the executive councils had seven members elected from within the administrative council. Besides their own weekly meetings, the district organizations met at the province level monthly with the provincial ladies' commission.

At the 'mahalle' or quarter level, the ladies' commissions, similar to the organization at the central party structure, had a fourteen-member consultative assembly. They had weekly meetings, and every month the quarter-level organizations met at the district level with the district organizations. At the level of the ballot box, 'sandık teşkilatı,' there were five members, including one chief observer, 'başmüşahit,' and four observers, 'müşahit.'

The Refah Party Ladies' Commissions throughout the country adopted this elaborate organizational structure. By the end of 1996, ladies' commissions had been organized in all the seventy-nine provinces of the country, if not in all the districts, quarters, or the ballot boxes. In the metropolitan areas of Istanbul and Ankara, the presidents of the provincial organizations prided themselves of organizing even at the apartment level. The Refah Party Ladies' Commissions were very well organized in a country in which entrenched parties had poor organizational capacities and could not find observers to supervise the ballot boxes in general elections.

The party elaborately and clearly defined responsibilities of these organizational branches and units. Minute descriptions were documented of the interpersonal norms that would guide the way the activists approached their potential constituency. The central party organization was careful to project a humane and tolerant image of the party. In the 1970s, when the Milli Selamet Party played a key role in Turkish politics, it was accused of precipitating polarization in the country with its radical and uncompromising stance as a coalition partner. In the 1980s, the electorate wanted to erase the memory of the cantankerous politicians vying for self-promotion and sweeping the country into the hands of the military. The new leaders of the Refah Party wanted to obliterate this image of an Islamist party. In order to reach a larger constituency than the Milli Selamet Party could, the Refah Party had to be able to approach those who did not share their ideology and draw them to their ranks. Under these conditions, tolerance and humility were important characteristics that the activists of the party were taught to practice. The work schedule of the Istanbul party organization used an imperative mood and emphasized, in its preface, the principles that were expected to guide organizational activity:

- Do not provoke hatred; provoke love
- Do not make things difficult; make them easy
- Do not be fearsome; be a deliverer of good news
- Do not be judgmental; be forgiving
- Extend greetings; there is grace in greetings

These common-sensical public relations guidelines were parsimonious, simple and authoritative. There was a messianic tone in the way they were articulated as if coming out of a holy text and as simple and authoritative in their call. They were communicated to activists who were to take part in the party organization before they began working for the party in Istanbul.[45] A similar message was given through the Ankara organization.[46]

The responsibilities of individual units within the organizational structure were as clearly and elaborately laid out. The Istanbul branch listed the prerequisites of a good organization, before describing the specific responsibilities of the different organizational units within the party. In order to become a "good organization," the party unit first had to employ qualified personnel. Then all the qualified personnel or the party functionaries had to be taught their duties within the party. Unity of belief and thought amongst the members was of prime importance. Conflict and contestation would sap effective action. United in their goals as well as thoughts, the members had to have affection for each other; affection would allow party members to love their institution and deepen their commitment to it. The party organization and different units in it had to be organized in a hierarchic manner.[47] Hierarchy would increase efficiency and allow for effective decision-making. The party aimed to have a paternalistic, patriarchal rather than a democratic, egalitarian organization. It would encourage protective ties and solidarity built by affective relationships. The guidelines also underlined that the well-being of the members of the organization should be taken seriously and the fact that they are a family should not be forgotten.[48] The analogy to the family was an appropriate one since the party organization expected from the party activists the allegiance family members are expected to have and the sacrifice they are capable of making in the context of a patriarchal organization in which elders are respected and younger people are taught how to become like the elders.

The booklet, which elaborated the principles of organization, emphasized that people who have independent businesses should build the party organization. Qualified personnel thus meant people who were qualified to spare their productive time to attend party meetings and partake in the activities of the administrative or executive councils. The party was careful to the minute detail of who could have the potential to commit himself to the party without a high opportunity cost.

The formal structure of an executive or an administrative council meeting was dictated to the prospective organizers. Every meeting was expected to be organized according to the following agenda:

- opening and roll call
- current issues
- issues which require consultation
- issues that require decision
- preparation of the agenda of the administrative committee
- programming activities
- supervising activities
- wishes and hopes for the future
- closing of the session.[49]

The party organization was keen to inculcate the members with a particular ethos and identity. In this endeavor, the party skillfully benefited from public relations or interpersonal communications techniques. The propaganda unit was essential in the party organization in which previously given public relations guidelines were elaborated and reiterated, accompanied with various psychological tips. Propaganda work

- had to communicate love
- should neither repel nor discriminate
- had to be convincing
- had to convey the truth about the party
- had to make things easier, not difficult
- had to make others love, not hate
- had to use soft language and avoid roughness
- had to be a messenger of good news, not fear.[50]

The brochure that was prepared to teach the party functionaries skills to approach the electorate emphasized the importance of a conciliatory style and positive thinking. In a country in which the primary secular majority had long been suspicious of Islamist politics, if not clearly threatened by it, this peaceful conciliatory approach was critical in enabling the party to expand its constituency. For many secular people, Islamists were against the Republic, illiberal, anti-secular, and were basically pre-modern conservatives. Besides, people in general were alienated from, if not intimidated by, politics, after the violent and polarized decade prior to 1980. In order to expand its constituency from the 7 percent of the 1987 election and appease the fears of the electorate, it was important and very appropriate for the Refah Party to move into politics in this pacifist manner, aiming not to antagonize or aggravate the people they approached. Our interviews attested to the female activists' commitment to these guidelines, as we shall discuss later. Islamist women were operating in a well organized, well run opposition party that closely guided the activity of its members in mobilizing others.

# Chapter 3

# Women in the Organization

Ladies' Commissions began to be organized around the female relatives of Refah Party men, but soon expanded to include women who belonged to very "different camps." Women who were brought up in a secular environment were appalled seeing other women wear headscarves overnight and, as if this was not enough, work for a party that upheld an ideology that would restrict one's liberties.[1] Only threats to or deception of the women concerned could explain these women's choices. Secular groups assumed that the Turkish state and society gave women autonomy and the opportunity to pursue their rights, which might not have been possible in an Islamic society like Iran.[2]

This chapter explores this assumption and the seemingly inexplicable manner in which women of the secular camp were drawn into the Refah Party. I trace how some of the women working for the party became involved. The women of the Refah Party set themselves apart from many others, not merely by covering their heads but also by deciding to work for an Islamist party that appeared to promote traditional roles for women. Although they had differences to be recognized, they also had similarities with many uncovered women and men that needed to be acknowledged. Refah women also sought to assert their autonomy at the same time as they created a community in which they could participate.

Thomas Franck, in his book *The Empowered Self*, argues that an individualist, " a person who sets out to choose the components of his or her own unique identity" is a modern phenomenon.[3] Before the modern age, according to Franck, "law, custom, culture and religion prohibited such self definition."[4] Communal rules and religious practices defined who one was and could be. In the modern age, however,

I would like to argue that even when there is a turn to religion, the "empowered self" asserts itself against preconceived definitions of what the individual should be or should do. The religious "individualist who sets out to choose the components of his or her own unique identity" perforates the boundaries of what religion would permit; in the process, he or she transforms the meaning of religion and how it is experienced in modern life.

The modern individual need not be a loner. The empowered self of the individualist seeks not merely self-sufficient independence, but rather relations of interdependence where he or she can seek "trust, loyalty, friendship, caring, responsibility."[5] Autonomous individualists are not, in the words of Mackenzie and Stoljar, "atomistic bearers of rights" for whom "values, social practices, relationships, and communities that are based on cooperation and interdependence threaten or at least compromise autonomy."[6] Relations of interdependence need not compromise autonomy or individualism. Refah women, much like other women of their age, sought both autonomy and self-definition in their turn to activism within a party that upheld a religiously inspired ideology.

Who were these religiously inclined, dedicated, industrious women that carried out the striking activism of the ladies' commissions? Why did the party appeal to them? What were the costs of aligning themselves with the party or with Islamism? In this section, I shall point to the range of backgrounds among the women who carried out these tasks and generate hypotheses to understand how and why they were drawn into the Refah Party. Because of the small size and unrepresentative nature of my sample determined by snowballing method, I shall merely draw attention to the variety that exists among women leaders who were affiliated with the Refah Party.

Most of the fifteen Refah women interviewed had presided over the party organization at either the province (four of them) or the district level (nine of them). The two others had presided over different administrative units, such as "organization" or "propaganda," within the commissions. All the "presidents" had worked at different lower-level units within their commissions before they presided over their respective organizations. Among those interviewed, eight women had university degrees; three were lawyers, two dentists, one a pharmachologist, one a graduate of divinity school, and another had a Ph.D. in Turkish literature. With the exception of two women, all had attended secular public schools. The high proportion of university graduates among those interviewed could be due to the snowballing method used to draw our sample. The people we asked for connections might have preferred to link us up with the more educated women of the commissions, because they wanted to represent themselves in their most educated selves. Or, the women we connected with initially were those in top administrative positions who were there possibly because they were well educated and these women were in closer contact with others who were similar to them in background. In either case, it is noteworthy that there was an incidence of highly educated women in the higher echelons of the ladies' commissions in the metropolitan provinces. All the women interviewed were married and had children.

These women came to work in the party ranks of their own will. Friends or people in their community influenced them, but there had been no pressure for them to become the activists that they became. A critical number among those in the top leadership positions came from secular backgrounds, not merely secular schools but also secular families, which supported Kemalist secularism.[7] The party began organizing women to modernize its cadres and expand its ranks and was only grateful to recruit women from these backgrounds. Among the women interviewed, there were basically three different paths through which they had traveled to the party organization. Some of the women seemed to be influenced by friends or teachers in the secular schools they attended. Others were attracted by the generosity and kindness that the party members exhibited toward them. A third set of women came from traditional families that were receptive to the Islamist call of the Refah Party.

## SCHOOL AS A SITE OF ISLAMIST INFLUENCE

A critical group of women, particularly among those in top leadership positions, came from middle-class families who were deeply committed to the Republican state and its secularism. These women received a secular education that prepared them for professional lives in the public domain. However, they were introduced to and influenced by Islam during their school years and decided to cover their heads according to what they believed Islam to dictate. Women wearing headscarves were barred from the opportunities that the Republic promised its educated women who understood Islam as the state did and did not cover their heads in public institutions. Consequently, there was a disjunction between what the education of the headscarved women prepared them for and the roles they could assume within their newly defined Islamist identity as citizens of the Turkish Republic. The Refah Party benefited from this dissonance and recruited educated Islamist women who could neither become the regular professional women that the Republic expected educated women to become nor could fit the image of the regular uneducated housewife. In turn, the headscarved women could find an opportunity with which they could use their education and skills to challenge the statist understanding of Islam and secularism. Consequently, they could use their skills to empower the pro-Islamic groups that sought power.

About one-third of the women in our sample (five women) belonged to this group who became interested in Islam because they were influenced by their Muslim friends or acquaintances at school. Three women were at universities when Islam attracted them. They covered their heads either after they finished school or during their school years and were embroiled in the headscarf controversy in the country. After they covered their heads, working for the Refah Party was their single important option for self-realization.

The fact that school was a site of Islamist influence gives credibility to the concern state officials have over the wearing and spreading of headscarves in the universities. Universities provide a medium of self-realization for youths who have just come of age to assert who they are and differentiate themselves from others. Before Islamism became the popular political ideology in the 1980s, students adopted leftist or nationalist ideologies in their university years. Yet, the prohibition against wearing headscarves had been ineffective amongst female students who were influenced by Islamist teaching that expects women to cover their heads. To the contrary, the prohibition sharpened their will to fight the system and define themselves in opposition to it. If forced to it, rather than take their scarves off, they were ready to drop out of school, though they did try to have both their diplomas and their headscarves.

Behind the recruitment of these women into the Refah ranks lies this determination to keep their headscarves. The women who covered their heads as students could not be integrated into "the system" with their headscarves, despite their educational qualifications. The secular state could neither provide a secular role model for them to emulate so that they would not make the choice to cover up nor succeed in integrating them with their headscarves into the broader secular system. Public education had unintended consequences: It could not socialize students to endorse the type of secularism the state legitimized, but it nevertheless provided them with the educational skills to challenge the state and its policies. With its restrictive understanding of Islam and defensive approach, the state narrowed the choices these women had, and pushed them to work for the Islamist Refah Party.

E. S. was a prototypical example of such a woman activist. E. S. thought that she was drawn into the party ranks, not because it was a premeditated goal, but rather a consequence of other choices she had to make after she was initiated into her Islamic worldview. E. S. was at law school, when she leaned toward Islam and covered her head during her third year. She came from a strictly Kemalist and secular family, committed to the Republican ethos, with its nationalism and statism. Her father was an army officer, a member of the institution most loyal to Kemalist reforms. She was a graduate of Üsküdar Kız Lisesi, an established, respected secular public high school for girls. The family traditionally supported the statist/social democratic Republican People's Party (RPP) founded by Kemal Atatürk himself. RPP had defined Turkish secularism and initiated the reforms to privatize religion. The party was in opposition to the center right Democrat Party-Justice Party tradition that appealed to the religious sentiments of the people. Her family and their party believed that the Justice Party exploited the religious sentiments of the people to get votes. All her family members fervently supported RPP's charismatic leader Ecevit in the 1970s, when Ecevit challenged the old RPP leader İnönü with promises of social democracy. E. S. recalled going to rallies to hear Ecevit, an eloquent orator. She had an interest in politics since those days.

The nature of this interest changed when E. S. began attending law school and confronted the headscarf problem at Istanbul University. When her classmates from Prayer Leader and Preacher schools who covered their heads were maltreated and denied entrance to their exams, E. S. was shocked. She had no headscarved friends before she attended university. She was uninitiated to Islam beyond a cursory exposure in her family and secular public school. However, as a young law student with social democratic values and particularly sensitive to questions of justice, she protested on behalf of headscarved students. Further protests followed. A few women with heads covered and a few others who supported them without head covers would gather in front of the university entrance; among them, E. S. stood out as a vocal advocate of the headscarved students. She protested not necessarily to propagate Islam or contest Republican secularism but rather to defend civil rights. When their protests came to no avail, she tried approaching political leaders whom she thought could change things. She had the political efficacy to do so. She decided to write to Ecevit, because she thought he believed in justice. She wrote more than one letter, and received no response. The secular leadership of the country chose to ignore the issue.

Only Erbakan, the leader of the Refah Party, paid attention to the call of the headscarved women and their advocates. E. S. clearly recalls Erbakan's visit to the university campus. She describes him as a messianic figure with a round, gleaming face that emanated peace. Erbakan promised to resolve the headscarf issue and allow headscarves in universities, when the Refah Party came to power. His announcement was a relief and a glimmer of hope for E. S. who had lost all faith in leaders she once idolized. The Refah Party thus became an attractive route.

Gradually, E. S. moved from being an outsider advocate of the Islamist women to becoming one herself. E. S. had always been interested in mysticism and Eastern philosophies. The daughter of an officer in the Turkish army, she had also always been a nationalist. When the works of Muslim intellectuals such as Ali Bulaç, İsmet Özel, and Abdulrahman Dilipak began to appear in 1986,[8] she was moved by their writings. She realized that "nationalism which had inspired her till then was not enough." She was proud that now there were some Turks who could contribute to the literature on Islam. In her pride, her nationalism asserted itself.

In 1987, she covered her head, despite the opposition of her family. She gave a fight against her family, and a year later she graduated from law school. Because her head was covered, she could not be easily employed. She could not take her bar exams in Istanbul. She could not be a court lawyer or work for the government. A year after her graduation, she made a hasty marriage to an Islamist man. Marriage to an Islamist man would secure her Muslim identity and liberate her from the surveillance of her disapproving, secular family, a development that women with similar experiences to that of E. S. shared. This was an autonomous choice unmanipulated and deliberate and about shaping her future life.[9] Yet, this was also a choice that would draw her into a web of relations or culture where autonomy was less valued and deference to hierarchy, including that of the husband, was the norm.[10] At a time when she felt like an alienated housewife with little opportunity for anything else, the Refah organization in Istanbul proposed that she work in their ranks to help establish the ladies' commissions. Her husband was working for the party and they knew E. S. had been an articulate supporter of the cause of covered women; they very much would like her to join their organization. She did, and found herself working intensely for the party organization, because she did not have an alternative. Secular institutions of the Republic could not accommodate a covered woman, so the party organization was critical for E. S. in realizing her potential and making use of her professional training.

In the ladies' commission, she could channel her political interests into effective action as she influenced other women, coordinated their activities, and generated power. She enjoyed the trust, friendships and collaborative atmosphere of the commissions.

The story of Ç. H., who was also drawn into Islamist ranks at law school, was perhaps more dramatic. She had to fight her secular parents, who opposed her headscarf and, later, her Islamist husband, who tried to restrict her autonomy. During the process, she had to fight a serious decline in her economic and social status.

Ç. H. was the youngest daughter of a "dava vekili," a person admitted to practice law and to conduct litigation in courts of smaller towns in the absence of professional lawyers. She characterized her father as a first-generation Kemalist who supported the Democrat Party that had come to power in opposition to the statist secularist Republican People's Party. She recalled her father wearing a hat in public, the kind Kemal urged his fellow countrymen to wear when he initiated the Hat Reform of 1927 and prohibited the wearing of the traditional fez, in the words of Bernard Lewis, "the last bastion of Muslim identification and separateness."[11] Yet, the family had preferred to support the Democrat Party against Kemal's Republican People's Party, because it was wary of authoritarianism and appreciative of the political liberalism—including more grounds for religious expression—the Democrats promised if not delivered. Ç. H.'s two elder sisters were both teachers, one an elementary school teacher, the other a high school math teacher in the secular public schools of the state. Ç. H. was the brightest of the sisters and graduated from the local high school as the first in her class. The father expected his youngest daughter to become a court lawyer. Before his retirement, he had been deeply disappointed; professional lawyers with law degrees had moved into town and he was prohibited from practicing law in his district. He hoped that his youngest daughter, with a law degree, would give him vicarious satisfaction and achieve what he himself could not.

Ç. H. decided to cover her hair at law school, in Ankara, after she became good friends with G. S., a Muslim woman who was covered. G. S., unlike Ç. H., came from a religious family where the father took an active interest in the religious instruction of his daughters and personally initiated them into Islam. The Republican reforms were more critically received by certain sectors of the populace than others, and it was difficult to uproot beliefs. G's father had been an active member of the Milli Selamet Party in the 1970s. At school, G. S. and Ç. H. discussed at length both Islam and why G. S. was covered. G. H. became a role model who was kind, intelligent, generous, and courageous for defying social pressure to go uncovered. Ç. H. sought to emulate her. With G. S., Ç. H. could discuss who she was and what she wanted to become.

Ç. H. bitterly disappointed her own family when she decided to cover her hair like her friend G. S. The family believed and tried to make Ç. H. believe that covering her hair would mean denying all her prospects for success and recognition. Ç. H. would not even hear of this success, because she had begun to hear a "different drummer." She bought her first headscarf and the subsequent ones secretly, with the money she saved from her meager allowance for transportation. She would walk an hour in rain to save money for her scarf. In response to the refusal of her family to accept her with a scarf, Ç. H. began hiding it. She would put the scarf on after she was a comfortable distance from home so she could not be seen. The family reaction grew violent but still futile. The mother destroyed the headscarves she found in Ç. H.'s handbag by throwing them into the stove. Ç. H. continued to walk, save money, and hide her scarves from her family. Having a long coat, a pardesü, was her next dream. G. S. helped Ç. H. acquire one through a relative who had given it away. Ç. H. recalled that her first pardesü was so ugly, so unfitting, and yet so precious to her. In her new outlook on life, she did not care for fashion or superficial looks but rather her faith. Once her decision to wear the headscarf was made, it was impossible for the family to change her decision. Ç. H. had opted for a new lifestyle, which dictated the headscarf and which, in turn, symbolized modesty, reserve, virtue, and obedience to God. She was asserting a new identity and differentiating herself from the generation of her parents, who were inspired by the Westernizing reforms of Mustafa Kemal and identified themselves with Republican secularism in which Muslim women went uncovered.

Ç. H.'s impulsive marriage to an Islamist man allowed her to avoid living with her parents where her scarves were burned. Her husband was an unemployed graduate of a veterinary school. Soon after her wedding, she was thrown out of law school, because of her headscarf, and she became homebound. She had a son. Her husband did not allow her to step out of the house by herself. He was a conservative Muslim patriarch. Furthermore, he did not hold a proper job for about eight to eight and a half years. With a son to look after, Ç. H. had to work long hours at home, sometimes packaging sugar, other times making decorative paintings that her husband sold at the outdoor market to earn the family income. They were so poor that when she was pregnant with her son, she recalled inhaling the smell of lamb chops that were cooked in the neighbor's house with craving and digging the garbage for some remnants, because they had no money to buy meat. In her parents' house, Ç. H. had to fight parental domination; at school, the patriarchal state; and now, in her own home, a patriarchal husband.

An Islamist network came to her rescue. When a friend who knew how desperate they were for work asked her if she would teach at a local Quranic course, she learned the Quran in one week to be able to teach it to others. That week, she recalled, she had the Quran in one hand, and a spoon in the other while cooking for the family. Eventually, she found a job at an Islamist women's magazine, and later in *Milli Gazete,* which was right across from the Refah Party Ladies's Commission quarters in Ankara. Friendships developed with the women in the commission, and they asked her to join their ranks. Her husband who by now had also found a job, agreed to her joining the party, and she willingly accepted the offer. She began working outside the home out of sheer economic need; however, once she began earning money, she began to assert her autonomy in the family. The husband who would not let her step out of the house gradually became a tolerant person who recognized his wife's autonomy. Ç. H. argued that when her husband restricted her movements earlier in their marriage, he was not the "real Muslim" that he later became. Even though she did not articulate it as such, Ç. H. was a liberal who respected individual freedoms. She believed that she gave a silent fight against oppression on all fronts—including in her parental family, in school, and in her own household—and won.

Both E. S. and Ç. H. had studied law and found it difficult to find a job with their headscarves. A. Ç.'s experience was different, because she had gone to the school of dentistry and could have a private practice with her degree and her headscarf. She shared an office with a male classmate and earned her living as a dentist. A. Ç., however, also began covering her head in the university and was also influenced by Islam in school. She also came from a secular, middle-class family, and she too had a serious confrontation with her parents, especially her mother, about covering her head. Both her parents were professionals, and her mother was the president of a bank branch. Like E. S.'s parents, they were fervent supporters of the social democratic Ecevit. A. Ç. was also a very bright student, one of the top three in her class at the Erenköy Lycee for Girls, an established educational fortress of the Republic.

Ironically, in this secular institution, A. Ç.'s history teacher was the religious role model who left an Islamist imprint on her. Once again, the secularizing Republican reforms had reached their limits in mobilizing the people, even among some who were to serve as history teachers in public schools. This history teacher served as a model of an upright, moral person who had faith. He was also a special teacher who would take the time to engage in serious discussions with his students and patiently respond to their questions as other teachers did not. A. Ç, always articulate and with a critical mind, was a favorite student of his who would often debate with him and challenge his ideas. The students knew that the teacher's daughters covered their heads and that he would take time to do his prayers during school breaks. Much as A. Ç. disputed her history teacher's ideas and beliefs, she was influenced by him and his religiosity. She decided to cover her hair after graduating from high school, while she was attending the school of dentistry.

At the time she decided to dress according to Islamic custom, A. Ç. did not even have a skirt that was below her knees. She had to dispose of her miniskirts and acquire long ones. Her mother was devastated by this decision and put up a big fight to change her daughter's mind about the headscarf. She was concerned about her daughter's future and marriage prospects. The mother claimed pejoratively that only a mufti or a pastor would marry her the way she dressed herself; she believed that her daughter would lose all her social status with the headscarf. She insisted that all covered women were marginalized in society. Despite what was exhorted to her, A. Ç married an Islamist activist who was a graduate of the Marmara University International Relations Department, rather than a pastor or a mufti. A. Ç.'s mother did not realize that Islamism was penetrating society, spreading among educated people and establishing its own social circles. People influenced by Islam were creating new channels of upward mobility and new communities of support.

A. Ç. earned more than her husband did and was quite independent of him in her private life. This model of a wife earning more than the husband did not quite fit in with the ideal division of labor many Islamists upheld, but reality asserted itself. Turkey's secular tradition, which had encouraged girls to be educated, inevitably left its imprint on its citizens who turned to Islam. As a believer who had financial security, individual autonomy, and flexibility of schedule in her professional life, A. Ç. kept in touch with other Islamist women. When some of her friends began working for the Refah Party, she offered to help them at the party organization before the elections. Once she began going to the ladies' commission, she found herself in the midst of responsibility and further commitment.

With the ascendance of Islamism in the 1980s, girls from secular backgrounds were attracted by Islam while they were being educated in secular public institutions. They were neither forced nor pressured to become observing Muslims. On the contrary, they were pressured not to cover their heads and had to fight to have themselves accepted with their heads covered. The secular role models were not as attractive as the Muslim ones; becoming a good Muslim meant becoming virtuous, just, and moral. They covered themselves, despite serious opposition, thus asserting their newly acquired identities in defiance of their parents, their schools, and their state. Their headscarves and long dresses set them apart from the secularized masses whose Western-inspired morality and norms they refused to emulate. Working for the Refah Party allowed them to realize themselves as good Muslim women. Their secular education had prepared them to assume responsible, professional roles within the public realm, and the Refah Party benefited from this preparation as it recruited these Muslim women with secular backgrounds into its ranks.

## THE PARTY AND PUBLIC RELATIONS IN RECRUITMENT

Other women interviewed joined the Islamist ranks because the party helped them and they were inspired by or indebted to the party. In this group, two women were introduced to the party through the National Outlook organization, an umbrella organization of the party in Europe. These women received help and benefited from the activities of the organization. The National Outlook organization, which was organically linked to the Refah Party, sought to recruit sympathizers and create a constituency among Turkish workers, in Europe. Turkish workers, particularly those living in Germany, resorted to the National Outlook organization not merely for ethical guidance but also assistance in solving problems of adaptation to survive in a foreign country. No other Turkish party had organized so extensively as to have an umbrella institution abroad.

B. A. had nothing to do with the Refah Party or what it stood for before her husband became sick and had to be treated in Germany. The couple went to Germany without knowing the language and without much money. They had no relatives or acquaintances there. Under these circumstances, the National Outlook members and organization, which lavishly extended financial and psychological help, welcomed them. B. A. gratefully explained that the people associated with the organization did not refrain from any assistance they could give. They had the husband hospitalized, they visited him there even though the hospital was outside the city center, they helped pay the hospital expenses, found a flat where he could recuperate with his wife, and after they were discharged from the hospital they looked after the couple. B. A. said that she could not think of any relative who could do half as much for her or her husband as these people of the National Outlook did. She had not witnessed the humanity "these people" exhibited anywhere else in the world. She was naturally obliged and deeply touched. She promised to herself that after her return to Turkey, she would work for these people. She was not one of them, as her continuous use of the term "these people" emphasized, but she was so affected by their generosity that she wanted to become and eventually did become one of them.

M. H. had a similar story. Like many other members of the commissions who assumed leadership roles, M. H. was brought up in a secular environment. She graduated from the well-known secular high school for girls Nişantaşı Kız Lisesi, situated in Nişantaşı, the fashionable, upper-middle-class neighborhood of Istanbul. After graduating from high school, she was married. The young couple went to Switzerland as guest workers soon after their marriage. M. H. had to adjust to a completely different environment and culture where she did not even speak the language. She had to teach herself German and then Italian, and she experienced what being a migrant worker meant. She recalled how her family raced after a car with an Istanbul license plate for two hours to hear news of their country and acquaint themselves with a Turk. Under these conditions, homesick and longing for her country, M. H. was introduced to the National Outlook organization. She began participating in its activities, in her words "as an individual with a social need, even though she was not in the political arena then." Her children began taking Turkish and religion lessons within the organization. She began attending its gatherings and establishing networks through the people affiliated with the National Outlook. Gradually, she became a leader actively engaged in the success of the organization. Turks who came as workers, she explained, were ignorant on so many issues, including health, consumption, and their rights to help and education. She could not resist offering to help them. Eventually, she became the president of the National Outlook women's commissions in Switzerland.

After their return to Turkey, she found domestic life unacceptable. She could not be satisfied exchanging recipes for desserts to be offered at tea parties, after all her years of work and social activism in Switzerland. Therefore, she volunteered to work for the Refah Party.

The decision was a culmination of her work in the National Outlook organization abroad.

## TRADITIONAL FAMILIES AND RECRUITMENT

More than one-third of the women we interviewed came from traditional, religious families that had proclivities to respond to a religious call coming from the public realm. Our interviewees told us that most of the women who worked in the party ranks came from this more conservative background. Among those we interviewed, there were women with fathers who had worked for the Milli Selamet Party and women who had husbands in the Refah Party. There were also women who attended local Quranic courses; one was a graduate of Prayer Leader and Preacher school. By the early 1990s, the women who attended these religious schools had increased in numbers.[12] The graduates of these schools were an important pool of potential party activists. Many of these traditionally religious women who were recruited to the party organization were young. They began working for the party after they graduated from high school when they were seventeen or eighteen. Their families would not consider sending them to universities. Working for a party that respected religion was an opportunity to keep themselves occupied in a legitimate vocation. The party thus tapped the religious proclivities of the population, channeled traditional women's needs for challenge, and politicized these women.

M. A. was not sent to school after elementary education, yet she attended the local Quran course for six years. She could read the Quran and, she believed, discriminate between right and wrong in religious propaganda. When she was eleven or twelve years old, she began wearing the "çarşaf," the loose black cloak that covers the whole body, not merely the head. She was taught at the Quran course that the Prophet Mohammad's people had to differentiate themselves from others, including in dress. "Manto" (the word for coat in Turkish derived from the French "manteau") that the majority of the population wears in Turkey, was an imported type of clothing from France. The Prophet, however, had advised that the Muslims keep away from everything that was of the infidels. M. A. believed in the Prophet and covered herself in her çarşaf with pride. Her family who had sent her to the Quran course approved of her attire.

Ironically, when M. A. married she took off her çarşaf. More effective than the teachings in the Quran course, however, were the expectations of her husband. The Quran also sanctioned obedience to one's husband. When she married, her husband did not want her to wear the çarşaf. Instead, he asked her to cover her head and wear a long coat. He believed that wearing the çarşaf was a stigma in social life. The person was branded as a reactionary and the people were repelled by it. M. A. obeyed her husband and began covering only her head.

M. A.'s husband worked in the Refah Party. He also came from a traditional family in which religion was important. One day M. A. found herself invited to a gathering by the ladies' commission. Everyone in the party circle knew her husband's family and their involvement with the party, and the occasion triggered her own engagement and involvement with the commissions. Even though her husband's party links gave her own commitment to the party some depth, she worked independent of him and rose within the commissions on her own. The party was thus extending its links from its male members into their families. M. A. felt that her own work in the party was approved of and encouraged by her husband's family, and knew that her mother-in-law was proud of her visibility in the ladies' commissions.

## PARTY WORK: SACRIFICE, FULFILLMENT, AND BOUNDARIES

As discussed before, women's recruitment to Refah was received with apprehension and dismay by large sectors of the secular population in Turkey. Their recourse to the party was seen as false consciousness at best, because it was seen improbable that women cover their heads and work for a cause that would restrict their rights and choices. Interviewing the Islamist women, we saw that they wanted to construct new identities for themselves different from the ones that their secular heritage had bestowed upon them. The fight that many, if not all, of them gave to assume these new Islamic identities allowed these women to claim an individualism that many of their secular sisters lacked. Many Islamist women challenged their parents' norms, customs, and religious practices rather than assume them at face value. Ironically, the self-definition of these women necessitated that they deny the way their parents worshipped. They followed a different path in which they covered their heads in observance of religious law, broadened their horizons, and had new options of self-realization. They could generate new relationships, new friends, and new communities where meaningful engagements and achievements could fulfill their lives. The party structure and the secular context in which they engaged in the politics of an Islamist party set limits to how far women could go, but they were nevertheless content to go as far as these limits.

All the women interviewed, without exception, emphasized that they worked in the party ranks for "God's sake": *Allah rızası için çalışıyorduk* ("we worked for God's sake"). This was a critical difference between women in the commissions and those who worked in other parties. Those in the other parties worked for their ideals, beliefs, ideologies, self-interests, cities, or countries. Even though "working for a cause" was their common denominator, perhaps "working for God's sake" lended itself to devotion and sacrifice more easily. Women received immense satisfaction from the work they did, but "working for God's sake" was their explanation for their committed work.

Religion was an effective means of political mobilization. It could prompt sacrifice from the people who believed in the cause and the party they believed to be promoting this cause. In the case of women, "working for God's sake" meant that they did not expect any mundane rewards such as elective or appointive office in return for their work. They insisted and were proud that they did not expect any worldly rewards. This attitude was crucial, because it relieved the central party organs from recognizing women's work in material terms. For the women concerned, it meant avoiding greater stress and confrontation that the pursuit of these rewards would involve. These women received profound satisfaction from the work they shouldered for the party, such that they did not seek further positions of authority and public recognition. They were content with what they had. They sacrificed for the party and in return, basked in its networks of solidarity, received recognition, and exercised influence and, circumscribed as it might have been, power. In the process, they were educated, an opportunity that they might not have had otherwise. They thus expanded their confined lives and their horizons, even when they had to accommodate a new set of confines set by the party and the context in which the party carried out its work.

Many of our interviewees related stories of the different types of sacrifices women made for the party. Not many of the women in the commissions had independent incomes. They were, even when educated, mostly housewives who were dependent on their husband's income. Those we interviewed had saved from the allowances their husbands gave them or used their skills in cooking and knitting to generate funds for the party. At times, working for the party meant hard physical labor in poverty. These conditions lent themselves to the evolution of myths that many of the interviewees basked in retelling. At least three women narrated the story of a poor activist, an orator who woke up in the middle of the night and baked bread for her family so that she could use her bread money to buy a minibus ticket to attend the commission's gathering. This story was also published in *Milli Gazete* that many of the Refah members read.[13] The newspaper coverage helped extend this theme of sacrifice that in turn helped invent and shape the self-image the commission ladies had of themselves. Similar stories of great personal sacrifice, such as women giving up their engagement rings or even selling their shanty houses, had circulated with among the women we interviewed. These stories of sacrifice were upheld as badges of honor that women were very proud to carry; they set the standards of self-denial and self-discipline that women adopted.

"Working for God's sake" meant hard work. Many women we interviewed explained that they prioritized party work before "themselves," their families, and children. This choice was ironic to the extent that Islamic teaching, it was generally argued, prioritized women's domestic roles as mothers and wives. Reminiscent of the famous Egyptian Muslim Brotherhood activist Zaynap al Ghazali,[14] these women were ready to trade off their responsibilities to their husbands and children for their work in the party. C. A. said that she would work until midnight, and at times a week would pass before she saw her son, who would be asleep when she arrived. She would come home like a guest. Others told how they would drag their children to party meetings and demonstrations. Ç. H. believed God would protect her children while she was working for the party, and she could neglect them in the process. With conviction, she told the incident of how her son survived falling into an iced pond when she had to deliver an important speech for the party. The younger members of her commission who volunteered to take care of her son brought him, all wet and shivering, into the room where she spoke. He did not even catch a cold, and the incident strengthened her faith that God approved of her work. In the ladies' commissions, it was common that women rotate amongst themselves the task of taking care of children who were brought to the meetings, because there was no place to drop them.

Cooking for the family was another task that the women who worked in the commissions had to squeeze into their hectic schedules. Almost all of them said that they cooked at night so that there would be food ready when they returned from party work the following afternoon. Women interviewed worked full time, at times 9 a.m. to 9 p.m., when they were in the party organization. Still, they did not neglect the demands of being proper housewives who served hot food to the family every evening. They did not complain; they merely planned ahead.

Working for God's sake and getting immense personal satisfaction from the work they did was quite independent of any spiritual or material rewards. As a researcher who had conducted research on and done extensive interviews with other women in politics, including parliamentarians and municipality council members of different cohorts and feminist activists of different persuasions, I was struck with the unmitigated pride and joy these women had in their political work. It was described as "very beautiful work" or an "exceptional experience" with a group of "exceptional women." Without fault, all women interviewed recalled their political activism as a success story, something neither the women parliamentarians nor municipality council members, nor even the younger generation of feminists, did. The commission ladies' joy and pride was a very worldly feeling. While they might have been inspired by religious considerations, their personal ambition and drive for power had set them on the road to success, and they basked in it.

For Ç. H., working for the party and being very successful as she was, was a means of claiming back the status she lost after she covered her hair and began moving into the Islamist ranks. She explained, "We all proved something; we gained status; we had been kicked around." Ç. H. had covered her hair, was condemned to house arrest, and, supposedly, could do nothing right. But party work, she said, "was a path for us. It was a path for us to prove ourselves to ourselves. It was wonderful to be a person who was needed. I did see many marriages begin improving when wives began working in the party." Ç. H. recalled how her own marriage and her status within her marriage improved as she became more and more engaged in the party work. Her husband, who had not allowed her to leave the house when they were first married, recognized her autonomy and authority. The woman who began working for the commissions assumed responsibilities, cultivated contacts, and developed programs. Her colleagues in the commissions began phoning her at home to reach her, ask her opinion, want something from her, and inform her. The husband, who picked up the phone, because phones always rang for him, discovered that they now wanted his wife. She was needed and respected by others; she was somebody who would be called upon. The husband would recognize this transformation and respect his wife that he used to take for granted. The mother in law, who had been a housewife all her life and assumed authority through her son, would see that now her daughter-in-law had another source of authority, independent of her status within the family as a mother or a wife. The ladies' commissions had many organizational units, and being one of the many presidents in the commissions might not have been that difficult a title to attain, but its impact on the status of the women concerned within her family was significant.

M. H. believed that her work in the party allowed her to educate herself. She said that she had a high school diploma, but she felt herself as educated as a university graduate, thanks to the political work she did. She learned how to organize activities, motivate others, and establish networks. She met many different people through her work in the party and learned from them all. Today she could knock on the door of a parliamentarian and contact him, ask a favor from him, invite him to her daughter's wedding: In her words, "this was a great success" for her. Her party membership gave her an identity like "a press identity card" that would open many doors. She could accost anyone with her status as a president of a Refah Party ladies' commission.

This sense of fulfillment was, ironically, also an obstacle to women's pursuit of higher levels of public office within the party organization. Women were disinclined to seek higher office, because they were content with what they were doing. Yet, there were also other serious patriarchal obstacles to how far women could seek higher positions within the party. Some of the most successful leaders did seek public recognition in return for their work in the party ranks. Sibel Eraslan, the successful president of the Istanbul province, or "the Refah Party woman who carried Tayyip to the mayoralty," as she was named by the press,[15] sought public office for her close circle after Tayyip Erdoğan became the Mayor of Istanbul. She was refused. Instead, she was "accused" of becoming like "feminists." The assumption was that women worked for a cause and were not expected to ask anything for themselves. Being a feminist was associated with being a self-promoter. Soon after, Sibel Eraslan and the women she worked with in Istanbul were to be replaced by a different cadre of women,[16] more subservient to the central organs of the party than Eraslan's group had been.

At least one of the women brought up the question of auto-censure in party work. M. A. said that she did not want to assume positions of public visibility as a member of the party, because she knew how merciless men could be in ridiculing the vulnerable. These women were successful, because they were socialized into the values of a "restraint" culture. They had learned how to discipline themselves and channel this discipline into commitment for the party. As such, they disciplined themselves to be content with the fruits of their labor within the commissions. They partook in politics on a parallel track to that of men's, one less important in shaping the future of the party, because they felt that men would not allow women to compete with men.

After the party was closed, the women of the commissions felt left out of the process of the formation of the new Fazilet Party. Women who were given the responsibility to institutionalize the new Fazilet Party ladies' commissions did consult the previous women leaders. However, the old cadres were left out of active engagement. All knew that there was concern within the Fazilet Party ranks that the party reflect a new beginning, a clean slate. Despite this concern, old male leaders, with the exception of a few, were actively within the new formation. Women did not understand why they were dismissed, as if the closing of the party was their fault. The most successful women who were so dismissed had in fact informally kept on making their weekly meetings. They protested to themselves that it was an unfair reward for their accomplishments. One woman said that she felt "like a mother separated from her children" when her organization was replaced by a new one. The men engaged in the party did not see women as authoritative partners in critical decision-making regarding the future of the party, even though they might have heeded women's advice involving the ladies' commissions.

Refah women followed different paths to the party organization. For some, coercive policies of the state and the illiberal environment at school or at home, particularly over the headscarf issue, precipitated the process of engagement with the party. For others, the lure of the active party organization and the help, solidarity, or the promise of an ideal community that its members extended was critical in recruitment. In either case, there was neither violence nor repression on the part of the Islamists who recruited women to their ranks. Ironically, secular repression or the defensive measures of the secular establishment in public or private life had the unintended consequence of making the Islamists more attractive. For those coming from traditionally religious families, as much as others coming from more secular backgrounds, becoming a party member and working for the party was a means of self-realization. Women enjoyed the mundane sense of empowerment that this process allowed them to have. They enjoyed the skills they acquired in working for the party and utilized the opportunities the party activism gave them to assert themselves in the public domain. They were very much part of the secular establishment, which encouraged individualism and individual empowerment usually associated with the Western modernism that their party allegedly rejected. They enjoyed the individual satisfaction they got from their work and basked in the opportunities they had for solidarity and comradeship.

One could take a critical stance regarding these narratives of self-fulfillment and claim that there were limits to opportunities women could have within the party's decision-making structures. There were very few women in the decision-making organs of other parties as well, not just the Refah Party. Nevertheless, one could argue that it would be easier to justify the exclusion of women in a party inspired by an Islamic ideology that emphasizes traditional roles for women rather than a party that upholds egalitarian values based on human rights. Considering the untraditional roles female activists played in the party, such a claim is difficult to make on theoretical grounds. Islam accommodated the public roles women assumed in the party. Yet, there is room for interpretation, especially because the male politicians in the party were traditional men socialized to uphold traditional roles. Public roles for women could be justified to the extent that they served Islam, and men knew what that extent was.

Without getting into arguments of "false consciousness" and making claims that "the Islamist women do not know their real interests" that are ultimately difficult to sustain without establishing an essentialist conception of the "right consciousness" and falling into the trap of cultural domination, another argument could be made as to why it was difficult for women to assume higher positions of power within the party. Women's contention that they were carrying out their activities for "God's sake" made it difficult for them to seek office in their own name. Seeking higher office was selfish. They could not pursue positions of power and expect inclusion in higher echelons of decision-making "for God's sake" in a context in which patriarchal men knew the better interests of all and all for "God's sake." Perhaps women needed more time and experience to seek higher office "for God's sake."

# Chapter 4

# Mobilizing for the Party:
# From the Personal into the Political

The women of the ladies' commissions enjoyed the work they did and were very successful in what they did. They recruited large numbers of women into politics and created a significant female constituency for the party. In a country where women were practically invisible in orthodox institutions of politics, no other party had this organization, drive, or success in recruiting women into its ranks. The Refah Party ladies' commissions could boast of hundreds of female members who were diligently mobilizing thousands of voters. The women of the commissions moved in uncharted territory. They approached women who did not share their assumptions or beliefs. They proved that if you approached women the right way, you could draw them into politics. The women of the commissions destroyed the myth that women were disinterested in politics.

In this chapter I examine how women of secular Turkey decided to support an Islamist political party that many believed would impose restrictions on secular lifestyles, and I trace how women of the ladies' commissions appealed to other women and motivated them to be interested in the politics of the Refah Party. I argue that the ladies' commissions were successful, because they discovered that the boundaries between the private and the political as well as the secular and religious were much more porous than assumed. Women of the commissions permeated these seemingly tight boundaries and tapped political energy from the female population confined to their homes. I shall begin my discussion by presenting a macro-level picture of the activities the ladies' commissions carried out.

## ACTIVITIES OF THE LADIES' COMMISSIONS

Women of the ladies' commissions carried out their activities within their tightly structured organizations. Even though there were twenty-five different functional units in the administrative councils of the metropolitan commissions, the activities of the ladies' commissions primarily revolved around "party organization," "propaganda," and "public relations" units represented in the executive councils. Education of the recruited members and orators who would work in the party ranks was also an important unit of activity.

Organizational activities involved institutionalizing the elaborate party machinery at different administrative levels of the polity. By the end of 1997, the metropolitan province of Istanbul, where most of this research was carried out, had 32 districts (*ilçe*), 37 counties (*belde*), and 863 quarters (*mahalle*) where there were 18,125 ballot boxes.[1] According to the ladies' commission report prepared for August 1997, the party was institutionalized in all districts of Istanbul and in 24 counties. There were 472 representatives and 500 vice-representatives in all quarters of the province. 1,490 chief observers (*başmüşahit*) and 2,137 observers (*müşahit*) were given the responsibility of overseeing the ballot boxes.[2] Progress report presented to the 6th Congress of the Party Provincial Organization stated that the women members increased from 158,287 to 377,888 between 1995 and 1997 in Istanbul.[3] The total membership, according to the same report, increased from 676,337 to 1,072,333.[4] Female members thus constituted about one-third of the party membership in Istanbul.[5]

The propaganda activities aimed to communicate the ideology, goals and principles of the party to its constituents. The party expected its functionaries to propagate its worldview and the solutions it offered to national, international, and local problems. The party activists were advised to engage in a series of activities and use various means, which included informal chats organized at homes and person-to-person talks called "full stop" visits (*nokta ziyaretleri*). In "nokta ziyaretleri," the party members got an appointment from a person targeted as a potential ally and visited her with a group of one to three party members to engage her in the activities of the party. The party members also organized video shows, cassette recorder sessions, indoor meetings, panels, conferences, forums, debates, and trips; wrote letters and greeting cards; presented small gifts; celebrated commemoration days; and provided social services and networks to propagate the party ideology within this context of social engagement.

The public relations activities aimed to cultivate relations with and extend ties to different social groups and secondary associations. Propaganda and public relations activities were similar to the extent that both emphasized developing personal links with the constituency beyond an attempt to explain what the party stood for. Public relations activities were carried out through visits to hospitals, celebrations of weddings and births, offering condolences, paying courtesy visits, engaging in social activities, and paying attention to the problems of individuals and associations, including political parties, administrators, professional associations, schools, and unions.

Besides the propaganda and public relations activities, ladies' commissions were expected to offer education to their members who worked in the party organization. A primary responsibility of the commissions was to educate their activists about the principles that guided party activities, the organization of the party machinery to which they belonged, and the party ideology, that is, the "National Outlook" they were expected to propagate. Yet the education of the members or the incoming activists was not limited to party propaganda or party work. The educational courses and conferences provided by the commissions covered a broader range of subjects and issues, including current political problems, human rights, independence and freedom, election law, public relations, human psychology, and the environment. The goal was to cultivate party workers and initiate them into politics and world affairs.

Work done by the ladies' commissions was, punctually and in writing, reported to higher levels of party machinery. Every month, the presidents of the district level ladies' commissions reported to the province level ladies' commissions as well as the district level of the central party organization. Similarly, the presidents of the provincial-level ladies' commissions reported to the representative responsible for ladies' commissions at the province level of the central party organization. These reports included not merely filling out the form distributed by the party organization but also a written assessment of the monthly activities. The provincial organization ranked the districts according to their success in organizing and carrying out different types of propaganda, public relations, or educational activities. The leadership aimed to encourage a competitive spirit of service to the party. For example, from a report for March 1992 prepared by the male representative of the ladies' commissions in the Istanbul central party organization, we learn that Ümraniye, Gazi Osman Paşa, and Bakırköy ladies' commissions ranked first, second, and third in recruiting new members by recruiting 238, 170, and 110 women, respectively.[6] In organizing educational seminars, the rank order changed to Üsküdar, Pendik, and Kartal commissions with 182, 10, and 9 seminars organized, respectively, and so on for different categories of ladies' commission activity. The same report also cited which districts were unable to recruit members and which districts failed to turn in their reports. A comparison was made with the accomplishments of the previous month, and it was reported that February had been a more successful month. We learn from the same report that letters of merit were awarded to those districts that were most successful during the year 1991. The report also cited in detail women's contributions to the campaign to help Bosnia, which was initiated by the Istanbul party organization. The reference to a gold bracelet, four gold chains, seven pairs of earrings, one Maşallah[7] gives us an idea of the deeply personal commitment the members had to the party and the Bosnian campaign it initiated. Gold bracelets and gold chains are given to women on various occasions, mostly weddings and births, or are bought by them as security deposits. Earrings are women's embellishments, and Maşallahs are expected to protect children from evil eye. Women were ready to give up these very personal possessions in an act of solidarity with women in their party and their religious sisters in Bosnia. In a times of crises, family members who did not see one another would come together to help those members in need.

Activities of the ladies' commissions were carried out with small funds collected from membership dues or events that the commissions organized. Women did not have the funds that the main organization had. Even though some of the leaders in the commissions were professionals earning incomes, many others were not or despite their professional education did not have the opportunity to work for money. The ladies' commissions primarily organized among housewives, women who had the time but not the money to support the party. The large sums of money that the newly emerging Muslim bourgeoisie had did not directly affect the activities of the commissions. Even though women themselves could raise the money they needed to undertake their activities, they relied on the central organization to rent cars and auditoriums or borrow videos. Women in the commissions had to ask men for help in organizing their larger projects that required some financial backing. This dependence was a cause for auto-censure when women had to decide on the activities they should engage in. Even though none complained about this financial dependence and, to the contrary, all emphasized how money was not important in their activities or how they could generate the money they needed, the few men we talked to were keenly aware that women did not have money. The men attributed part of women's lack of authority in the central organs of the party to this economic weakness. Nevertheless, this issue did not restrain women from building strong ties of loyalty and interpersonal networks of solidarity among women.

Using their meager funds, the women carried out numerous activities with success. The Progress Report presented to the Sixth Congress of the Party cites the following list of activities carried out by the ladies, commissions between 1995 and 1997 in Istanbul:[8]

| | |
|---|---:|
| Number of members recruited: | 219,601 |
| Educational seminars given: | 3,465 |
| Conferences organized: | 1,572 |
| Video shows organized: | 1,564 |
| Home chats organized: | 14,231 |
| Weddings organized: | 2,656 |
| Engagements, circumcisions: | 750 |
| Condolence visits made: | 4,215 |
| Visits to celebrate newborns: | 3,740 |
| Visits to artisans: | 6,325 |
| Full stop (nokta) visits: | 156,415 |
| Visits to the sick: | 12,625 |
| Tea chats organized: | 18,628 |
| Visits to hospitals: | 12,325 |
| Courses given for girls to acquire skills: | 1,600 |
| Picnics organized: | 310 |
| Visits to schools: | 760 |
| Trips to theaters: | 210 |
| Fairs (kermes) organized: | 75 |
| Extensive investigation (tarama): | 22,460 |
| Indoor meetings organized: | 326 |
| Quarter's Consultative Council meetings: | 471 |
| People reached: | 1,226,575 |

Activities of the ladies' commissions received frequent recognition from *Milli Gazete* that had organic ties to the party. The newspaper reported on the conferences, panels, visits to hospitals and state officials, educational seminars, social services, and social activities, including commemoration or celebration activities of the various ladies commissions in the country. Most of the news items were self-congratulatory, uncritical reflections on work done. The party thus propagated the accomplishments of the commissions and gave legitimacy to their activities. The fact that Halise Çiftçi, president of the Ankara organization, one of the most successful ladies' commission presidents at the province level, was on the staff of *Milli Gazete* enhanced the organic ties between the party and the paper and facilitated the flow of information.

Looking over the articles published on the ladies' commissions in the *Milli Gazete*, one could see the wide spectrum within which the commissions defined their activities. For example, the visits organized by the Public Relations branches included not merely hospitals, flood victims, and social service institutions, but also visits to the Social Democratic Populist Party minister responsible for Women and the Family, or a visit to the Afghan Embassy,[9] a visit by Sakarya Ladies' Commission to the Association of War Veterans (Muharip Gaziler Derneği),[10] or a visit to the Foundation for the Protection of Mothers of the Martyrs (*Zübeyde Hanım Şehit Analarını Koruma Vakfı*) a foundation initiated by the True Path Party.[11] The ladies' commissions were careful to cultivate ties with the women of the parties they competed with, such as the Social Democratic Populist party and the center-right True Path Party. While the women in the commissions never had a brokerage role between their own party and its adversaries, contacts with competitors helped build a conciliatory image, not merely for the ladies' commissions but also for the party.

The ladies' commissions reflected the party line and the National Outlook ideology in their public conferences and interviews. The oppressive nature of the headscarf ban was a favorite topic that was brought up frequently in almost every meeting the ladies' commissions held. Female leaders referred to their personal experiences of victimization through this ban to cultivate solidarity with covered women in their constituency and condemned the ban as oppression.[12] The ban prevented Muslim girls from following the tradition of the Prophet who advocated education and claimed "one should study science even if it is in China."[13] To highlight the predicament of headscarved female professionals who could not practice their professions, an experience that many leaders of the commissions shared, the Ankara Province Ladies' Commission organized a meeting with the headscarved lawyers. The lawyers drew attention to the restrictions that the bar association imposed on headscarves despite the innocence of their headscarves.[14]

In their public statements and speeches, the members of the ladies' commissions were also careful to emphasize that their organization did not discriminate against uncovered women. They portrayed themselves as members of a tolerant organization that was open to people with different beliefs and practices, unlike the secularists who lacked tolerance and attacked believers.[15] In order to grow, they had to recruit women who were uncovered. With this consciousness, they positioned themselves against gender discrimination. They emphasized that they were against exploitation because of gender and wanted to protect human rights.[16]

The ideal Muslim woman publicly depicted by the leaders of the ladies' commissions was a "mother/fighter." That mothers were sacred was emphasized with references to the Prophet's sayings and the Quran. Both these sources expected women to be respected and revered primarily as mothers. Muslims accepted that "Heaven was under the feet of mothers."

Yet, as Muslim women, the commission ladies argued, they were partners sharing a common cause with their husbands. President of the Ladies' Commissions Süheyla Kebapçıoğlu explained on various occasions, "Muslim woman should not see herself as a dishwasher or a cooking factory or a child-care provider. Women in Islam are not the maids of their husbands but rather confidants and friends in battle. During the "Golden Age of Islam," women participated in battle along with their husbands and accomplished important deeds."[17] This did not mean that Kebapçıoğlu accepted feminism. She argued that as Muslims they could neither see women as completely equal to men—for example women could not have the freedom men had outside the house where their extramarital affairs were tolerated—nor lower women to second class status. Men and women, she argued, "completed one another"[18] in their common cause.

In constructing the image of the mother/fighter, the women of the commissions frequently alluded to history. They expropriated figures from the Ottoman Turkish tradition to bolster their cause and cultivate the ideal of the Muslim women they aspired to in the present age. Some of these historic figures were mothers of heroes, generals, and great leaders. President of the Kayseri Provincial Ladies' Commission Hayriye Yalnız addressed a congregation of partisan women gathered in the city stadium as "Mothers who have given birth to Prophets, *Yavuz Sultan Selims and Fatihs,* those who have caused the world to be liberated, welcome."[19] Yavuz had conquered Egypt and brought the Caliphate to the Ottomans. Fatih had triumphed over the Byzantine Empire. The Ottoman heritage was thus expropriated to affirm its Muslim identity. Secular tradition ironically prided itself with the fact that Fatih was a cosmopolitan ruler who appreciated Western art and crafts (he had his picture painted by the Italian artist Bellini) and Yavuz was a Muslim leader conquering fellow Muslims. Sibel Eraslan, the head of the Istanbul Provincial Ladies' Commission, also addressed her female constituency gathered in a fashion show organized by the Istanbul commission as "you, each of whom will be mothers giving birth to future Fatihs."[20]

In acclaiming historical figures, the women of the commissions also referred to heroines who fought in Ottoman or Turkish wars. Nene Hatun,[21] who had fought with courage against the Russians in Erzurum during the 1987–1988 war, was one such figure. President of the Ladies' Commissions Süheyla Kebapçıoğlu addressed 300 women from Kütahya, Manisa, and Çanakkale gathered at Balıkesir with the following words, "*Nene Hatuns and Kara Fatmas*, women who carried shells in our national war of independence and fought in trenches are not yet forgotten. Women who cooked in the trenches, carried water on their backs, wrapped the wounds of the wounded, and who thus wrote epics are our women. Women who worked in the trenches in times of battle now have to be part of our country's development by propagating and partaking in cultural activities."[22] Sema Arslan, who was responsible for the Propaganda Activities of the Yenimahalle district of Ankara Ladies' Commission, addressed the congregation of women who attended an appreciation dinner organized for the women working in the party organization with the following words: "In our war of independence, we had grandmothers who sacrificed their children to protect the shells. Today, in the present day Turkey of the twentieth century, it is you, the Nene Hatuns who introduce the party to the people by going from door to door and claim the votes trust into ballot boxes for the Refah Party, for the right and the just."[23] The women of the commissions used the language of battle and compared their activists to heroines of war to build up their self-image.

The allusions to war used in public speeches and similar to the language used by men in the party were predicated on a bifurcated worldview. The women along with men assumed that there was a confrontation between them and the state, the East and the West. In their public speeches, the women of the commissions were not afraid to get into polemics, which they avoided when they approached prospective recruits to the party. President of the Ankara Provincial Ladies' Commission Halise Çiftçi crystallized the confrontation between the two camps as follows: "This system forces our people to make a choice. They have cut out a citizenship shirt. You have to wear it, whether it is tight or large for you . . . If your identity as a believer comes out, than you are thrown out of the military. The one who is a believer cannot enter school, because she is wearing a scarf. You will either be a believer or a citizen." Consequently, Çiftçi argued, "Either your religious days (holy three months and the religious "kandil" days) will prevail or those who have decorated this country with bells to celebrate the new year will. . . . Our grandfathers went to Europe to conquer it, but now this regime is going to Europe to become its slaves."[24] The lines between the believers and others were drawn by who celebrates what and were bolstered with the claim that Europe was exploiting Muslim Turkey.

Within this worldview it was argued that Islam had given more rights to women than the secularizing Republic ever did. The Prophet and his caliphs protected and valued women. However, in Turkey, in the name of freedoms and women's rights, women were exploited. They were degenerated and became tools of advertising. In the name of modernization, women's rights recognized by God (such as respect for women) were not given to women.[25] Divorce rates increased because the sanctity of family life disappeared. The women of the commissions distanced themselves from the achievements of the Republic and criticized its westernization the way the male leaders of the party did.

However, they were very much part of this Republic. President of the Istanbul Provincial Ladies' Commission Sibel Eraslan ended one of her headscarf criticisms in which she blamed the oppressive order for preventing her from practicing law, even though she was a lawyer, with the comment, "Are you afraid that the Republic will disintegrate with a 90 cm scarf? God willing, it is again us who will not have the Republic torn away. The Muslim woman who is chaste and honorable will not have this Republic torn away."[26]

Even though most of the public forums or discussions initiated by ladies' commissions seemed to aim at confrontational party propaganda, some were more sophisticated. On Human Rights Day, conferences were organized on human rights by the Ankara Ladies' Commission[27] and by the Sarıyer district of Istanbul. In Ankara, guest speakers included the presidents of the Ankara and Istanbul ladies' commissions; representatives from Mazlum-Der, an association founded primarily to defend the rights of covered women; Bosnian Solidarity Association; and Human Rights Association. In Istanbul, the Sarıyer commission was able to bring together an even broader spectrum of participants, which included a member of the Republican People's Party, lecturers from Boğaziçi and Marmara Universities, feminists from radical women's groups, a member of Turkey's Association of Disabled, journalists, and representatives from Mazlum-Der and the Human Rights Association.

The parameters of debate in these conferences were nevertheless limited. The Islamist participants primarily argued for expanding the rights of Muslims, specifically on the headscarf issue and the importance of observing Islam to prevent human rights violations. The rights of Bosnians, Chechenians, Afghans, Palestinians, and Southeast Anatolians also surfaced in the presentations. In line with the party ideology that emphasized the importance of cross-border Muslim solidarity, Islamist women, including those from the ladies' commissions, extended themselves in solidarity with the plight of other Muslim women. The issue of Kurdish women, which guest lecturers brought up, penetrated their framework of debate primarily shaped by the headscarf controversy. On Human Rights Days, the representative from the Human Rights Association, for example, criticized the closing of the pro-Kurdish Democratic Party (DEP), which was made possible by the collaboration of the Refah Party with the government then in power. The representative suggested, "Yesterday DEP was closed, today the closing of the Refah Party is in the agenda. Unless we raise our voice to these acts, we condemn ourselves to moral pressure."[28] Refah women thus allowed the fact that "defending human rights involved going beyond rights for oneself" to be voiced in their platforms. By and large, women we interviewed were uncomfortable if not apologetic about their party's lack of support for DEP. However, only a few of our interviewees explicitly denounced their party's collaboration in the expulsion of the DEP representatives from the parliament, even though they all condemned the closing of their own party. The women of the commissions mostly felt that they had to accommodate the practices of their party before advocating human rights.

Educational seminars were given on a wide range of issues. Male party elites played an active role in those seminars, which initiated new activists and members to the party. The seminar organized by the Central Organization of the Ladies' Commission in Ankara for the purpose of training members who served in ladies' commissions was attended by about 300 women from around the country.[29] Prominent party leaders, including the head of the party, Necmettin Erbakan; the president responsible from Public Relations, Şevket Kazan; the president responsible for Electoral Works, Rıza Ulucak; the president responsible for propaganda, Recai Kutan; and the president responsible for the Party Organization, Ahmet Tekdal, all addressed women prior to the local elections, briefing them about the responsibilities of their respective duties and the party ideology. President of the Ladies' Commissions Süheyla Kebapçıoğlu toured the country to give seminars in different provinces,[30] explaining and propagating the principles and guidelines of their organizational work. Besides informing women of the activities and responsibilities of the ladies' commissions, she included explanatory notes on the role of women in society and in Islam to enlighten and educate her constituency.

The ladies' commissions did not merely teach their members and activists the workings of their commissions or the ideology of their party but also trained powerful orators, women who could address and influence others. All the women interviewed emphasized the critical role female speakers played in their organizations. When the education unit of the provincial organization in Ankara organized a forty-five-hour training session on oratory techniques, Ayşe Şahin, the president of the unit, explained that their aim in organizing the course was "to train women who could best communicate their feelings and thoughts, divulge the secret talents in us, and learn to speak effectively in front of different groups of people."[31] In educating their orators, improving their diction, and teaching oratory techniques, Islamist women crossed boundaries of their own rather narrow professional circles to recruit experts from the secular ranks. To empower themselves, they were ready to concede to the superior knowledge of the "secular camp" when it was needed and seek professional help.

## MOBILIZATION AT THE GRASS ROOTS: FROM THE PERSONAL INTO THE POLITICAL

Ladies' commissions mobilized at the grass-roots level. The women who were given the responsibility to establish a new commission and who had some ties to the party through husbands, relatives, or friends first contacted the people from their close circles. They approached the wives of the male elites from the central party organs. They inquired into the social fabric of the district and established who was who. They made a special effort to locate and develop friendships with women who were well liked, respected, and played a leadership role in the community. E. S. explained that they tried to locate the Perihan Abla, Sister Perihan, of the neighborhood, the popular heroine of a television series about life in an idealized middle-class neighborhood in Istanbul. Perihan Abla knew the people in the community intimately, socialized with them, and helped and advised them. Women of the commissions would approach and befriend the Perihan Abla and ask if she would organize a tea party for her friends so that they could be introduced to the neighborhood. The tea party would then be reciprocated in another friend's house. These social gatherings provided the backbone of the ladies' commissions' mobilization activity in a new quarter. Women of the commissions would reveal their political identities in the context of these friendships; however, they were careful not to preach, let alone be polemical, in these social contexts. They could be polemical in public meetings organized for their constituency, but not when they were approaching women they were trying to recruit. Over time, when the members of the commissions organized tea parties, there were occasions for explaining the ideology of the party.

It was crucial not to intimidate women they did not know with an alienating political rhetoric or with religious preaching. Instead, the ladies' commissions aimed to keep political activity within the confines of the social. The laywomen who worked for the party felt uncomfortable themselves with an overtly political discourse. For many of these women, political talk meant leftist talk, and leftist talk was intimidating. In an interview with one of the female commission members, I referred to the ladies' commissions as an "örgüt," a word that literally means an organization but has been commonly used in reference to the militant leftist groups. She was most disturbed. She corrected me that there was no "örgüt" around, that the word "örgüt" brought shivers down her spine and connoted the violence-prone Marxist Communist organizations which had victimized the youth. These female commission members, however, had familial relationships with people in their districts. They talked about the problems they shared, whether it was the high price of food or problems in schooling their children. Women from the commissions carefully cultivated these social relationships. They became emotionally linked to their constituency and moved them into the political domain. The social domain was not merely a venue to the political but also constituted the latter where these social networks were preserved.[32]

In these networks of friendship and solidarity, party ideology or its leadership was of secondary importance. One of the presidents of the Istanbul organization explained, "It was not Erbakan, it was us who endeared the women to the party and for whom they came to the party." Women of the commissions related to their constituencies with a civility that the latter could not find anywhere else. In Istanbul, the newly migrant population of the city appreciated the concern with which the Refah women approached them, responded to their problems, extended personal care and help. The commissions integrated the marginal groups to city life through their services and made the voices of these groups heard at the provincial and national level through their votes. Tea parties were not the only means of approaching new women. The women of the commissions systematically knocked on doors. In euphemistic language, this was called the "tarama," "extensive investigation" method. The members of the commissions literally investigated homes within their neighborhood, one by one. Kadıköy was an established, traditionally secular, important, district of Istanbul that was difficult for a pro-Islamic party to draw votes from. One of the presidents of the Kadıköy commission explained how they toured in neighborhoods they were responsible for and, eventually, challenged other parties in a district in which no one from the secular camp would have believed would get Refah Party votes. Women in the commissions prepared detailed maps of each street and house in their district. Usually five or six representatives from the commissions, including the president herself, would tour and contact the families in the designed neighborhood. Kadıköy had apartment buildings, rather than private houses or shanty town houses. The team from the commissions would knock the door of every flat, on every floor. Two party representatives would begin on the top floor, the other two on the ground floor, and the president would pick the remaining floors. They worked during the day, when housewives would be home and men would be away.

They would knock on a door, introduce themselves, and ask the lady who opened the door what she thought of the Refah Party. Next, they asked if she would consider or, depending on her previous response, "ever consider" voting for the Refah Party. If the answer was a "no," they would ask what she thought was wrong with the party and what the party should or should not do. They would listen carefully and assure the speaker that they noted her concerns. Even when some people closed doors in their faces, or men chased them out with dogs, there would be many who had the time to be polled. When they were not dismissed, the representatives would ask if they could enlist the woman they visited as a member. The first reaction would usually be a "no" or a "why?" Then the representatives would explain why they wanted to make her a member and why it would be advantageous for her to become a member. There were three important reasons. First, the party would like to forecast how many votes it would get. Second, the party would like to develop organic links with its constituency. Third, and perhaps most important from the perspective of the prospective member, the party would like to help its members to establish a community; if the member was in need of anything, they wanted to extend help. This help could be material or moral. It could be extended in cases of sickness, death, birth, or weddings, as the situation demanded. It could be the provision of health or child-care services or contributions to their daughters' dowries. The women who worked in the party generated this help locally. It was a continuation of the local "imece" (*collaboration*) tradition of collaborative work with which the women were familiar.

Members of the commissions noted women who did not want to become members but who nevertheless seemed amenable to persuasion. Over time, the commissions worked on such cases with particular attention. They arranged what they called "nokta ziyaretleri," visits made on an individual basis. One or two party representatives would try to get an appointment with or ask if they could come over for a coffee with these women that they had marked as prone to influence. Over coffee, they would socialize and develop friendships. The new candidates for party membership needed to trust established members, and after such friendships were secured, the women often wanted to join the party.

Local rites and traditions that had their roots in Turkish religious or cultural settings played a critical role in the activities of the ladies' commissions. As discussed earlier, the Republican reforms had aimed to privatize religion rather than abolish it. Even though observance of Islam might have changed and weakened in the lives of large sectors of the population, particularly in urban areas, traditions of commemorating births, deaths, and even marriages were still intimately inspired by religious practice across different groups, including class or region. Particularly when the commissions could not arrange for social visits or home chats, they would benefit from the opportunities for social contact provided by traditional customs, most of which were religiously based. Traditional readings of the Quran, particularly on holy evenings such as kandils, were always occasions the ladies' commissions capitalized on. During the Mevlud kandils, they helped the neighbors organize the chanting of the nativity poem, "Mevlud," written by Süleyman Çelebi, depicting the birth of the Prophet. When there were funerals, some families wanted to have the whole Quran read. Others wanted Yasin, the thirty-sixth Sura of the Quran, read forty times, and again the ladies' commissions were ready to organize these services. Middle classes within the bourgeoisie, the bureaucracy, or the intellectuals, who were all committed to Republican secularism, observed such traditions and most often the reading of the Quran after the funerals. Yet, these groups were too divorced from the religious realm to carry out these activities within their secularized niches. In this context, the Refah Party members offered services, established contacts, and empowered themselves. They allowed these secular groups, which included famous singers and stars divorced from religious discourse by practice yet committed to it by tradition, to maintain connections to religious traditions. Thus, they served a functional need, and acted as a buffer, linking the secular to the religious and allowing for their coexistence and dialogue.

The commissions took organization and provision of such religious services very seriously, because, from their point of view, these occasions could serve as access points in their mobilization activities. Friendships began developing in these contexts, and they could thus get opportunities to prove how faithful, committed, and caring their community was and draw other women into their circles.

Besides strictly religious traditions and rites, secular traditions women observed were also very useful to begin enlarging the ladies' commissions circles. There were the traditional "kabul günleri" reception days organized mostly by middle-class housewives in cities or towns, among friends and neighbors on a regular basis. Each woman would have a set date when she would expect her group of friends to come over. These tea parties where women gathered weekly, biweekly, or monthly were an important network of information and solidarity, which could be co-opted by the Refah women. Over time, the traditional *kabul günleri* caught up with the demands and needs of consumption society and evolved into "altın günleri" or "gold days," where women gathered money among themselves, and bought a gold coin to be given to each one of them in turns. Their savings thus generated local capital that could be used at their discretion.[33] Refah women attended these networks and introduced political issues such as inflation, corruption, and lack of local services, which were essential problems in women's daily lives and which duly resonated. The female Refah members were merely offering a political channel to tackle these problems in a context in which there were no closer alternative proposals.

Thus, the women of the commissions could locate what was political in the private realm of women and transfer it as such into the explicitly political domain. The private realm was not merely the realm of interpersonal relations that had political implications, as feminists had long discovered and encapsulated in the dictum "private is political." Rather, the private realm harbored immediate material concerns that were political in nature, even when they were not named as such, and had serious implications in the formal political domain. The interpersonal relations women of the commissions cultivated in the private realm became channels through which these political concerns could be carried onto the political realm. The women of the commissions located the medium in which women, including the party workers, felt comfortable, and moved them into politics within that social context. In the process, they tapped the traditional texture of the polity and politicized it as other women had been unable to do. Traditional rites and customs thus acquired new functions, which allowed women to have access to a political voice. The women of the commissions perforated the boundaries of the private realm at the same time as they expanded those of the political realm. Concerned with the sacred and their right to practice a more orthodox Islam, they initiated an unorthodox incursion into the heart of secular politics.

*Diversity and Recruitment*

The ladies' commissions were very careful to recognize the different needs and demands of local contexts. The Refah Party, unlike its competitors, was very successful in responding to local culture and the particular demands of the local constituency.[34] Despite its hierarchic, disciplined structure, the party allowed for flexibility among its branches at different levels of organization. Different province and district organizations were careful to respond to various socio-economic and cultural realities of the local contexts. In metropolitan cities, the party began organizing from the outskirts of the city where the new migrants lived in shantytown areas, capitalizing on a discourse of victimization and the promise of justice. In central Anatolian towns, it appealed to a conservative Sunni Muslim constituency with a traditionalist discourse. In southeast Anatolia, it appealed to the indigenous Kurdish population with a discourse of Islamic solidarity.

The ladies' commissions followed suit. In Istanbul, in the newly established, poor neighborhoods of migrants, such as Bağcılar, Sultanbeyli, or Ümraniye, the party workers would talk about lack of services, and communicate their awareness of material needs:   roads not built, schools not opened, health clinics unavailable. In more established, traditional and "richer" (as one interviewee described it) districts, such as Fatih or Üsküdar, issues of morality such as of prevention of alcoholism, prohibition of prostitution, hazards of western imitation, and corruption of national culture would be brought up. In the more fashionable, westernized upper-middle-class area of Caddebostan that was part of Kadıköy district, the commissions organized a fashion show of Islamic clothing in the famous casino Maxim, where popular singers and stars performed and gave concerts. They calculated that they could draw women disinterested in the Refah Party merely because of curiosity for the casino and the fashion show. Once there, these disinterested woman would develop sympathies for the Islamist community or, at least, would hear a few words about their work. The Islamist women were patient and could then cultivate these meager sympathies.

In certain districts the commissions were more successful than in others. In Istanbul, for example, the Çatalca, Yalova, Şile, and Kadıköy districts were most difficult to penetrate. In these strongholds of secularism, the boundaries of the religious realm were sharply crystallized over time and confined to how the Kemalists defined it. People were reconciled to their needs and values and had no motivation to question them. In the shantytown areas that harbored disillusioned migrants, the women of the commissions were more successful in recruiting members (as had been the case for the party in general). In these contexts, values and moralities were in flux, because people had been uprooted from their lands. The material needs were great. The rhetoric of the Islamist women resonated with the culture of the migrant population.

In Ankara similar attention was paid to differences between districts. For example, commission activities and discourse in Çankaya were very different from those in Yahyalar or Çantepe. Çankaya was the established, upper-class heart of the city where the president resided. Yahyalar and Çantepe were poorer, newly developed regions. The president of the Ankara provincial organization explained, "People were fed and clad" in Çankaya. There, one could talk about economic policies, the inflation rate, and issues of human rights, and bring in statistics and examples from abroad that the people in Yahyalar would not even listen to. In Yahyalar, people were fighting to survive; they had dire needs for food and coal.

It was not merely what was said that had to differ but also mannerisms and dress. The commissions knew that in Çankaya people celebrated secular holidays such as the New Year with more zest than they celebrated religious holidays. The women of the commissions arranged their public relations activities accordingly and prioritized the celebration of these secular holidays. They believed that in order to change people, first you had to accept them as they were and respect their views; otherwise a dialogue where they could generate sympathy for their cause would not take place. The orator who went to a house in Çankaya to celebrate Mother's Day would dress in a suit more like the way the majority dressed in the district. She would not wear the long Islamist coat, "pardesü," let alone a "çarşaf,"which probably connoted obscurantism for the majority of the population in Çankaya. Instead, she would wear a long suit. Her headscarf would be smaller and less obtrusively tied behind the back. She thus dressed according to what she believed was the correct Islamist attire at the same time as she adopted aspects of the secularist clothing of the people she tried to recruit. This was their means of permeating boundaries between the Islamists and secularists through dress codes.

In her language, she would be careful to use words that were "pure" Turkish rather than Arabic. When the Republic was established, the Kemalist founders undertook a major language reform in which they replaced the Arabic alphabet with a Latin one and established the Turkish Language Institute to purify contemporary Turkish from its Ottoman influence. Speaking pure Turkish delivered the message that you respected the reforms and their goals; you were no threat to the Republic. Thus the female representative of the Refah Party would greet the people upon whose door she knocked with the phrase "iyi günler" (*good day*), rather than "selamünaleyküm" (*let God's grace be upon you*), which was commonly used among the more traditional or religious groups in greeting one another. During my interviews, I noticed that the women of the party spoke to one another over the phone, or when someone entered their house, with a language that had more Ottoman words than would be customary for women of their age who had the secular schooling they did. The Refah representative working in Çankaya thus communicated that she spoke the same language that people who lived in Çankaya did and was also one of them, not someone to be afraid of. She did not see this as hypocrisy or scheming but rather as recognition of the different worlds to which people she tried to recruit to her party belonged.

Those interviewees who had experiences in other areas of Turkey besides the metropolitan centers narrated similar stories. They had to respond to changing agendas and shifting priorities as well as the diversity of entrenched local identities. E. S. recalled having to talk in Nevşehir, a small city in central Anatolia, about the problems of Southeast Anatolian border closings, because the Turkish truck drivers were detained at the borders and a large constituency of their wives needed consolation. This issue preoccupied the women concerned more than anything else, and the party representative had to respond to or integrate this problem in her contacts in the region.

A dramatic example of different priorities the commissions worked around could be observed in the Black Sea region. After the disintegration of the former Soviet Union, Russian women began coming to Turkey for prostitution. The large-scale operation of prostitutes in the northeastern Black Sea coast of Turkey led to a radical challenge of the prevailing moral code and the position of women within the traditional families of the region.[35] In Turkey, there were severe sanctions against female premarital sex and adultery committed by women. In contrast, male premarital sex and male adultery were tolerated. This double standard in the moral code provided fertile ground for prostitution. Under these conditions, local women from traditional families were threatened when their men began spending time and money with the prostitutes, at times deserting their wives to be with the prostitutes who became their lovers.

Refah women did not miss the opportunity to mobilize around this issue. In the district of Bulancak, in northeast Black Sea region, the ladies' commission of the party organized a campaign in which 6,500 signatures were gathered in support of a petition that protested the Russian prostitutes for undermining family life in the region. *Milli Gazete* printed, on its first page, a big picture of the woman who was the president of the commission in Bulancak and the head of the much-talked-about campaign. The president of the commission, Adile Gündoğdu, was a woman with eyeglasses and a çarşaf that barely left her eyeglasses in sight. She argued that now the parliamentarians had to show sensitivity to the issue if they wanted to preserve family life in the Black Sea region.[36] In the province of Trabzon, there was a similar campaign in which the president of the ladies' commission, who was similarly photographed in a çarşaf, explained that they had gathered 20,000 signatures in their province, which they would present to the governor and planned to take it to Tansu Çiller, who was at the time the prime minister of Turkey.[37] The commissions organized political meetings in which they put up posters that protested the Russian prostitutes: "Otel—Motel—AIDS" (Hotel—Motel—AIDS) and "*Turizm değil rezalet*" (It is not tourism, but disgrace).[38] Strikingly, this political activism was taking place in a context in which there was no tradition of women politicizing the problems they had as women and raising their voices in the public arena. Women's traditional strengths and talents in the private realm in organizing and shaping values were transformed into a political presence in the public arena when they felt their worlds were under threat. In due time, the Refah Party dramatically gained votes in the region.[39]

Activist work in different parts of the country was different not merely in terms of the issues addressed and the flexibility of discourse the different commissions adopted, but also in the relative autonomy women activists had as women in the public sphere. Women working for the commissions in Eastern Anatolia were much more constrained than those who were working in the Western provinces. Even though investigating a variety of provincial organizations was beyond the scope of this work, those women who had the experience of working in the East emphasized that the conditions were much more confining for women there. Patriarchal norms prevailed deeply in the East where women deferred to their husband and depended on them more than their counterparts in the West. M. H., who knew the commissions in

Diyarbakır, Bitlis, and Van, argued that the women working for the commissions in these provinces were much more dependent on their husbands for permission to do so. In her words, "There was no problem in Istanbul, but in the East the woman could not walk out without her man beside her, nor enter into public places, and attend seminars and meetings without her husband's permission. These taboos and criteria were kept intact. But thank God, in Istanbul we undermined them." It is understandable that women working in metropolitan areas would be more independent than their counterparts in the East, where traditions retain a stronger hold. M. H., ironically, thanks God for the autonomy she has in Istanbul. Her autonomy might be due to many factors, for example, the deeper level of secularization in the West. However, M. H.'s God is one who approves of women's autonomy if not delivers it.

Mobilization of the ladies' commissions proved that despite the prevailing assumption to the contrary, women were interested in politics. Religiously motivated, intensely committed women recruited other women by accepting them as they were, that is, as housewives located in the privacy of their homes. Approaching these housewives in the social context of their private domains, the women of the ladies' commissions could act as catalysts, channeling women's interests and demands into the political arena.

To the extent that the women of the commissions were left outside the decision-making organs of the party, one could expect that the interests of those who were mobilized would be difficult to meet and translate into politics. It has been claimed that women thus mobilized were merely boxes of ballots for the party instrumental in empowering a conservative elite. The party clearly benefited from female voters. However, it is doubtful that a mobilized electorate, male or female, could be contained without accountability for long. It would be presumptuous to assume that women could be manipulated and their vote merely used instrumentally for long. The barriers that exist and the patriarchal attitudes that keep women from higher echelons of the party need to be articulated, but with due respect to women's right to shape their priorities. Moving women to the political realm might have been a first step toward expanding their boundaries where they might better pursue their interests.

# Chapter 5

# Worldviews of Refah Women

The women of the Refah Party had a unique worldview that imbued them with the power they had to shape their community. In this chapter, I probe into this worldview. How these women think and what they believe in is interesting considering that they grew up in a secular context and yet endorsed a politically driven Islamist ideology. For many in the "secular camp," within and beyond the local context, these women were inscrutable, because they turned their backs to all the opportunities the westernizing secular state and society offered them and instead upheld an ideology that was against women's interests.[1]

Ironically, what Islamist women believed in was assumed to be inscrutable as well as self-evident and threatening. The secular establishment took measures to suppress them. Banning the headscarves and closing the Refah Party were part of these measures. Yet, what these women believed in was neither self-evident nor inscrutable. One had to ask and find out what the women of the party at the locus of this "threatening ideology" believed in. What did they believe about Islam such that they became the "other"[2] for the secular groups? What did these women, who worked with such commitment, think Islam entailed? Did their Islamist beliefs contradict liberal human rights, as is frequently argued?[3] Was their Islam a threat to secularism? What did they think of the headscarf issue? Did they think, as many people in the secular camp did, that their party obstructed their upward mobility within the party hierarchy?[4] Responses to these questions can shed light not merely on what Islam means for those who practice it ardently, but also how liberalism penetrates or coexists with allegedly conservative beliefs. Debates on multiculturalism and democracy frequently make important assumptions about the groups that are difficult to integrate with liberal societies, including Islamist groups.[5] Trying to understand what Islamists believe might be a step toward expanding democratic inclusion, if not solving all the theoretical tensions between Islam and democracy. Dictates of secular law and principles of liberal justice, including civil rights, might be more deservingly applied if we know what the excluded think.

To appreciate the way Refah women think about Islam and their experience in their party, we need to emphasize that these women grew up and were primarily socialized in a secular polity. Both those who came from traditionally religious families and others who came from staunchly secular families received at least their primary or secondary education in public schools. In Turkey, the 1924 Law on the Unity of Education prohibited religious teaching and allowed for state supervision over education. Under these conditions, Prayer Leader and Preacher schools operating at junior and senior high school levels,[6] which covertly propagated a religious ideology, were under the supervision of the secular state. Through their secular schooling, the women were exposed to an Islam legitimized and understood by the state where head covering was not an issue. It was assumed that a good Muslim girl need not cover her hair. Yet, secular education did not inspire all students with its ideology,[7] and alternative channels of socialization resisting the statist version of Islam also existed. Traditional families were keen to teach their own understanding of Islam to their children. A range of books, mostly written by people who had little learning of Islam, proliferated on the subject in the 1980s. Some teachers of the Prayer Leader and Preacher schools,[8] Quran courses, or friends also provided alternative understandings of Islam to the one the state practiced. The women picked up through these alternative channels that, for example, according to Islam, they had to cover their heads. With these mutually contradictory understandings of Islam, the women of the party had to reinvent themselves as Muslim women living in a secular country and working for a pro-Islamic party that was critical of state secularism. They had to accommodate the tensions that inevitably followed.

Probing into the worldviews of these women, one could see that the polarity that was set up between the secular and the religious groups could not be sustained. Refah women borrowed from the secular cultural baggage they were brought up with in constructing the Islam they believed in. Ironically, the Islam secular observers of Refah women depicted was diametrically opposed to the one the women themselves believed in, while both sides claimed they knew what Islam was really like. There were differences in worldview and perception of Islam among Refah women, just as there were shared grounds and ideals with secular women.

While the believers insist that there is one true understanding of the Quran, there have been different readings in practice. Islamic discourse on women also changed over time and place, as different Muslim societies institutionalized Islam through law and custom. Historians and social scientists have documented how there have been different readings of Islam leading to various debates on the subject. Some have shown how Islamic law concerning women contradicts dictates of basic human rights, while others have contested such interpretations and explained these dictates of the Quran in socio-economic contexts.[9] Fazlur Rahman, who argued that women's inferior status that has been written into Islamic law is a result of social conditions rather than the moral teachings of the Quran, had a constituency in Turkey.[10] Turkish jurists of Islamic law were influenced by or sympathetic toward his approach to questions of gender equality.[11] Some of the women interviewed had heard of and even read writings of Fazlur Rahman or those influenced by him. In this work, however, I am interested in the perceptions of Refah women regarding Islam and what they understand from it, rather than in an academic discussion of Islamic discourse. I shall now discuss how this group of Refah women who were introduced to conflicting views of Islam through their different agents of socialization responded to it all to recreate their own worldviews.

## RESISTING THE SECULARIST PERCEPTION OF THE 'OTHER'

The women interviewed shared the concern and the conviction that they and their party were grossly misrepresented by the secular camp. The self-image of almost all the women interviewed was shaped with this perception. They were anxious to communicate how they viewed themselves as opposed to how they thought "the seculars" perceived them. Islamist women wanted to show that they were different, but also not that different from the "others." Many of the women were uncomfortable with the question about their party's reflection of Islamic norms regarding women. They insisted that the question was irrelevant because their party was a party of the Republic of Turkey and not an Islamic party. Without exception and even though there was no such question, the interviewees insisted that their party was represented through blunt distortions and unfair characterizations in the media.

Some of the women who came to the party from the secular camp admitted their own biases prior to their membership. They were

keen to show by their personal example that the secular camp cultivated negative feelings against the Islamists. Ş. Z. explained how she
had been prejudiced against the Refah Party before she began making
friends with some of their members and later joined their ranks. She
had voted for the left-of-center hero Ecevit when she was nineteen
years old and worked both in the Republican People's Party and later
in the center-right Motherland Party. At the time, she would not have
believed her ears if someone had told her that she would work for the
Refah Party one day. She had blonde hair, she wore tights and open
sandals, and she was an assertive woman. The typical Refah woman,
assumed to be submissive, had a dark or neutral-colored long coat,
modest outfit, and head cover. Ş. Z. believed that the Refah Party was
presented as a bogeyman, "öcü" in Turkish, and a party of fundamentalists who were against secularism. Under this influence, she had
been furious when the Refah Party struck a coalition with the nationalist right to be able to get enough votes to pass over the electoral
threshold in the 1991 elections. She felt that even the nationalists were
less dangerous than the fundamentalists.

Despite the resentment she felt toward the party, she became
friends with some of its female members, which led to her eventual
membership and work in the party. When she got to know the people
who worked in it, her idea of the party totally changed. These were
honest, hard-working, committed people who accepted Ş. Z. the way
she was, with her tights and her blond hair uncovered. In the Refah
Party, she did not endure any of the disappointments and petty fights
involving self-promotion that she witnessed in the other parties she
worked for. Ş. Z. felt that the party was unfairly represented and
worked with a vengeance to have that image changed.

D. N. was also a woman who covered her hair late in life. She
had worked as a nurse in Germany for many years, uncovered, wearing green nail polish if she was wearing something green, pink if she
wore pink. Yet, all those years she had also longed for the voice of the
muezzin calling Muslims to prayer. When she returned to Turkey
she settled in Konya and began working for the party. She now had
the chance to satisfy her longing for the religious community she had
missed abroad. She was quite close to the female members of the
party leadership. Her son was engaged and attending university in
Ankara. In a visit to her son, she took the fiancée along with her to the
family of Şevket Kazan, a prominent party leader. D. N. proudly explained how the fiancée, who did not know where she was going, was
shocked when she found out that they had been to Kazan's family,
because it was so "modern." She recalled the dialogue verbatim: "The

fiancée asked, 'Mother you are living in Konya; how come you know this family in Ankara?' I said, 'Well, my daughter, you know of Sevket Kazan—well, this is the family of Sevket Kazan. The woman I talked to was his wife. The woman you talked to was his sister in law.' The fiancée was shocked and retorted, 'No . . . There cannot be such a family among the Refah people. I thought you were just an exception (both modern and Islamist)' . . . There you go . . . This was a family of women fashionably dressed, with makeup, dyed hair, cultured, and educated—people who wanted to live this world and the other world properly. Do you have to be a reactionary to be a Refah person? The other side (meaning the secularist camp) stigmatizes us with this image. We respect them; they should respect us!" D. N.'s model Refah family was modern, and modernity was linked with dress and makeup as well as education. Even though she did not explicitly state it, these characteristics were linked with western norms. D. N. did not specify what fashionably dressed was, but one could assume she meant following western fashion rather than the emergent Islamic one, which is not how most Refah women dressed outside their homes. It was obvious she approved of a "contemporary" (inspired by the West) image with makeup and dyed hair and wanted to refashion another's perception of the Refah women with this image. She at least insisted that these images were compatible.

B. H. was not as prejudiced against the Refah Party before she joined it. When we went to interview her at her home, she was dressed in bright yellow pants and a tight-fitting white blouse with bright yellow and green daisy patterns on it. She wore sandals and had let her long, honey-colored hair loose. Other covered women we interviewed did not always take their scarves off during the interviews. To the extent that the dress code was a significant issue in the lives of Islamist women, B. H. was certainly no different than any woman in the secular camp who was keen to follow western fashion. Her outfit cried it out loud.

B. H.'s family had all been followers of the center-right politician Demirel and his predecessor Menderes. Even though she came from a traditional family, she discovered Muslim culture and Islam late in her university years. A traditional Turkish family was typically secular, not Islamist, but growing up in her family, she did not acquire a bias against a pro-Islamic party. However, she personally experienced discrimination after she covered her hair. Thus, she knew the stigma that head coverings and the Refah Party carried within the secular order. She decided to cover her hair at the end of her university years. After covering her hair, she became an outcast. She had to sever ties with her friends; she could not go to the places she used to go before she was covered. She made a love marriage to her husband, a class-mate from college, but her husband told her that he wished she had not decided to cover her hair, because his family would not accept her with the hair cover. For eighteen years, the duration of their marriage, his husband's family did not accept her.

She knew that working for the party scared many others. Her neighbors found it hard to believe that she was from Refah, because their image of Refah was a negative one and they liked B. H. and her family. In our meeting, B. H. expressed her disappointment with me as well, because when I phoned to get an interview from her, I had told her that I wanted to get to know her and her colleagues. She said, "Are we from Mars? You want to know me or us, because we are different. Well, we are the children of this country just like you. We are not different. What needs to be understood is that we do not need to be understood as different. What do we have that needs to be understood as such? We see the same films you do, spend time in the same places you do, eat and drink the same things. They do not un-derstand us and call us reactionary. Well, we are not; that needs to be understood. I know students who come from your university are al-ways surprised to find us the way we are; they just have a wrong image and mistaken view of who we are." B. H.'s insistence that they, as members of the Refah Party, were like others reflected her revolt against the polarization in the country between the secular and the religious groups. Yet her persistent denial of difference also revealed the differences that did exist. She had decided to cover her head and work for the Refah Party because she felt that the party was unlike others; the implication was that "others" were not as good or moral. These actual or perceived differences were transformed on both sides into representations of one another approved by neither side. In all cases, the debate over perceptions hinged on how Islam was under-stood. What did the adherents of the party think about Islam and its rules concerning women?

## THE MEANING OF ISLAM AND ITS DICTATES ON WOMEN

Our interviewees who insisted that they were not that different from other people had their particular views on Islam and its dictates on women. These ideas were, substantively, not that different from the ones idealized in the secular realm. Refah women had formed their ideals and understandings of Islam and an Islamist worldview by borrowing from the secular order they were part of and the secular education they had received. They had thought less about Islam than one would expect from people who had made the kind of commitment they did to a pro-Islamic party, but their ideas reflected the similarities in values and norms they shared with men and women within the secular polity.[12] As such, the ideology of Islam that the women of the party had was in fact different from that attributed to them by many secular groups. While the responses of the women interviewed exhibited ambivalences, ambiguities, and contradictions, at the same time they reflected the particular socialization these women had and the secular context in which they lived.

Our interviews aimed to probe into the opinions of the interviewees on the question of women's rights in Islam. The argument was proposed that women's rights in Islam on issues of polygamy, divorce, court witnessing, and inheritance were biased against women; Islam encouraged the traditional division of labor between men and women that restricted women's options. Welfare women refuted these arguments. Their responses, however, revealed their widely varied understandings of Islam. Some believed that Islamic dictates regarding women were misunderstood and they did not restrict women; others claimed they were misunderstood, because there were no such dictates. Most were vague in their responses to the question or were disinterested.

Regarding the traditional division of labor between men and women, one common response was to affirm its existence and deny its inegalitarian nature. Many Islamist thinkers have argued that men and women are equal before God as believers, but that there exists a complementary division of labor between them.[13] The uninitiated mistakenly considers the complementary division of labor as unequal treatment. This argument was prevalent in the responses of many interviewees. The interviewees claimed that Islam might have encouraged a traditional division of labor but that being responsible for different tasks was not unfair. When they were reminded that these tasks were valued differently and the tasks women were responsible for lacked the power and prestige men's had, we were reminded that for God they were of equal worth. Our simplistic conception of power prevented us from recognizing the value of women's work and the power women had in the tasks they carried out within this traditional division of labor. The believer could understand the justice and fairness of this division of labor and these particular laws. Arguments of equal worth that material feminists once used were carried out of the secular realm on to a sacred one in a paradigm of religious belief where God was left to judge what was of equal value.

B. H. ardently defended the Islamist division of labor between men and women. She had earned a master's degree and a Ph.D. in Turkish Language and Literature from the Faculty of Literature in Istanbul University as she raised two children. According to B. H., Islam accepted marriage as a contract between two parties. Men were responsible for managing the household financially and women were responsible for housekeeping, cooking, and caring for the children and the husband. This was the principle, and it worked in practice. She was satisfied with this arrangement and with what her husband could bring home. She never shopped; her husband brought the food and the groceries and gave her a weekly allowance, which he increased when he thought was right. She was a person who was raised to be satisfied with what she had, so she never asked for an increase or for new clothes. Her husband would take her and their two children before religious holidays, *bayrams,* or when the new season arrived to a particular Muslim shopping center near where they lived and tell them to choose what they would.[14] When she wanted an appliance or expensive gadget for the house, she expressed this need. Her husband would not accept it immediately. In B. H.'s words, "beni terbiye eder"—he would humble or educate her, but eventually it would be bought. Her will would prevail in the end, even though she would have to wait and pursue her needs in a circuitous way through her husband. She did not approve of the consumption-based society and its consumer culture around her. She had trained herself to be happy with what her husband could afford. She was a successful political leader outside her home; at home she insisted upon claiming power the way women traditionally did, through men.

B. H. claimed hers was a liberating bargain with her husband. She was left with the freedom to do what she wanted to do, because she did not have to work outside the house to earn money once she fulfilled her duties to her husband and the family. She did not need to tend to the telephone bill, the electricity bill, the grocer, the butcher, or the market. She could pursue her interests, do what she wanted to do, engage in politics, and prove herself in the public realm of the party. The "realm of necessity" within this worldview was not any more the realm of housekeeping and family but rather where the money was earned in the public realm. Money earned in the public realm helped maintain the realm of politics. She let her husband cater to this realm of necessity, while she tended to the political realm where she could define herself and pursue her interests. She thought other women were not, in her words, as "free" as she was to do what they wanted to do. They could not leave the house at 9 a.m. and come back at 5 p.m. in pursuit of politics. "Why should she want to have this burden when she could be more free this way?" she asked. In turn, she was not like other women who minded handing a glass of water to their husbands or ironing their shirts when they wanted. Tending to her husband was merely an instrument for her to prove herself in the public realm. The traditional division of labor was thus substantively redefined, serving a functional purpose for her to become the public figure she had become.

B. H. endorsed the traditional division of labor in the family at the same time as she insisted on her right to pursue a public life. This choice had its ambivalences, which were duly accommodated. When we talked about her children's response to her work for the party, she said that they did not like it. She worked for the party, despite their disapproval. She defended her choice to her children by explaining to them that it was her *right*. She had looked after them all these years (they were, at the time, both in high school), educated herself under difficult circumstances and now, with her diplomas, "what would she do 'sitting' at home?" It was neither fair nor possible for her with her credentials and achievements to be just a housewife. The accommodation of these two potentially conflicting worldviews in the life of B. H. was striking. She defended the Islamist division of labor as vehemently as she defended her need to prove herself in the public domain and "use" her education for a public good. It was suggested that the traditional division of labor, which meant financial dependence of women on men, could give men the power to curtail the freedom women could have in the public sphere; however the suggestion was irrelevant for her. A good Muslim man would allow his wife freedom as long as she fulfilled her duties to him. As in various other interviews, B. H. also relied on the "ideal Islam" argument to counter criticism coming from "outside" the Islamist framework. She had cultivated a contract with her husband in which she lived the Islam she believed in at the same time as she secured her autonomy in the public realm. The concept of "ideal Islam" helped legitimize her contract.

Ironically, B. H. was one of those women who acknowledged there were limits to how far women could have power within their party. She realized that despite their hard work, women had no say in central decision-making organs of the party. When the new Fazilet Party organization was being founded, no one asked their opinion about who the central party organization should appoint as the president of the provincial party organization. When we suggested that perhaps women did not have the financial clout men had within the party, a suggestion which was made by a male member we interviewed, she admitted this could be a consideration. In retrospect, a defense of a traditional division of labor propagated through Islam coexisted, despite potential contradictions, together with a liberal political concept of individualism in which human beings realize themselves in the public arena.

According to C. A., Islam did not promote a traditional division of labor. This was a claim that those who did not know Islam maintained to oppress women. C. A. was a dentist with a private practice, and she believed that working outside the house did not contradict Islamic dictates. Her husband had a degree in Public Administration and worked in the Istanbul municipality run by the Refah Party. She earned more than her husband, and they both worked for the party. Her husband would help with the children when she put in long hours at the party quarters. She argued that women were victimized in the name of Islam without any Islamic grounds. As an example, she mentioned her male colleague with whom she shared her private practice and who did not allow his wife to work outside the home. It was alright for him to work together with a covered Muslim woman, but he himself would not let his own wife do the same. C. A. thought that women who allowed themselves to be victimized like this were at fault. She believed every individual was responsible for herself and should not allow herself to be exploited. Allowing oneself to be exploited by others, she claimed, had nothing to do with Islam. Her rhetoric resonated secular feminist arguments.

Not all women were interested in the subject of Islamic law regarding women. A. N. was the daughter of a preacher and prayer leader employed by the state. Raised in an orthodox religious family, she began wearing the "çarşaf," the black attire covering the whole body, at the age of twelve. When she married, her husband preferred that she just cover her head, because he thought the çarşaf was a stigma, and so she took it off. She deferred to her husband's wishes and she approved of the Islamic advice that men manage their homes and take financial care of their families. She proudly explained that she never shopped and her husband brought everything to the house, including the curtains and the furniture. Similar to H. B., her endorsement of this traditional division of labor did not preclude her from endorsing women's work outside the house and a woman's right to autonomy. She said, "Well, what if she works modestly outside the house? I am not against women working outside the house; if you are working morally under the circumstances of the day, there is nothing wrong here. You cannot compare the times the Quran was delivered with these days." Hers was a very pragmatic approach to Islam, reminiscent of Fazlur Rahman's arguments.

Despite her father's religious background, she was uninterested in scholarly arguments on the subject.

While she approved of the traditional division of labor between men and women, and was ready to make exceptions, she did not concern herself much with dictates of Islamic law. They were neither relevant to her life nor of theoretical interest to her. One would expect that her father, a professional preacher would inspire her with religious curiosity, but that was not the case. She was quite uninterested, or rather trustful of God, concerning laws like polygamy and unequal inheritance. When asked what she thought on these dictates, she said that she could not explain these issues clearly to us; she was no jurist herself and that we should ask these questions of jurists.

She could, however, be opinionated. She further explained herself, saying, "Well, which women would want to be one of four wives and struggle to have this realized? What is prescribed is just one wife, and people do not know this. Because they do not know, they just invent stories—like Islamists will force all women to be covered and be a co-wife. Never and never could the One who created men and women make them unequal." Hers was a deeply felt trust, based on her instincts of self-preservation and experience in a secular country, that God simply would not make unfair laws. Her common sense told her that no woman would like to be a co-wife; she decided that God, who knew best, would not let this be. She could afford this trust in the context of a secular Republic.

A. N. firmly believed in women's right to autonomy independent of their husbands. When she became the president of the ladies' commission in her province, she organized various campaigns to mobilize women into politics. To enlarge her constituency, her mother suggested that A. N. should go to the village their family came from and ask for votes from the women there. They had their ancestral home in the village, and some of their family still lived there. A. N. had been thinking about it, but she was disheartened. Her village traditionally supported the Justice Party, and one of her uncles was an administrator for the True Path Party, which replaced the Justice Party. She mustered up her strength and went to talk to the village women who gathered in the home of one of her aunts. She told the women that they were the ones working in the fields and they were the ones who were earning their own bread while their men sat in the coffeehouses, so they should choose the party that was the best for their interests on their own rather than vote like their husbands. The village women asked her what A. N.'s party emblem was like and she told them there was a plait of grain and a crescent. The women who tilled the soil identified with the grain and the rhetoric of power and autonomy that A. N. introduced. The uncle sulked when he realized that she had come to the village for political propagation, but they all accepted it eventually. In the elections, there was an unexpected turnout of votes from the village for the Refah Party. A. N. had succeeded in convincing the peasant women to vote for her party by appealing to their right to choose the party that served their interest because they were the ones who worked for their own food. Ironically, this is the same woman who argued that Islam expected men to bring the food home. She was ultimately a woman who empowered herself by working for the party outside her home. Her work outside the home gave her the autonomy she had with which she could appeal to the peasant women and with whom she shared pleasures of work outside the private realm of the family. Within this worldview, Islam expected women to respect their men but allowed women to get on with their own autonomous lives. In the secular context of the Republic and where there was no rigorous, unitary Islamic teaching, women who had been expected to work outside the privacy of their own homes set the cultural meanings attached to Islam that was practiced. A. N. was concerned with pursuing her own life and relationship to her husband, legitimizing certain aspects of her daily life with references to an Islam she practiced, and legitimizing others with reference to a secular code where work gave license to autonomy independent of what religion said.

A few women who had a wider knowledge of Islamic rules argued that the so-called restrictions did not actually restrict women, if Islam were practiced as a whole. Partial and random focus on certain laws that were taken out of their holistic Quranic context gave those people who did not know the Quran the impression that these dictates restricted women. Yet even these more knowledgeable women who felt that the Quran was misread had reconciled to and were influenced by secular modes of life.

G. S. came from a conservative religious family where the father took a personal interest in educating his daughters on Islam. G. S.'s father taught her about what Islam meant, what its dictates were, and what the Islamic intellectuals thought. G. S. attended public schools and was educated to become a lawyer, but, unlike many others who worked in the party and were not interested in what Islam said regarding inheritance rights, she also considered herself knowledgeable about Islam. As a lawyer trained to defend her cause, she consistently defended women's rights in Islam. First, she insisted that she was a believer, which meant that she had faith in God and what God said through the Quran, independent of its rationale. She did not need to seek justifications for why certain laws given in the Quran were as they were. However, if I requested functionalist explanations, which for her were insignificant, she could give some.

She argued that Islam scared secular women, because they decontextualized Quranic dictates and picked on some selectively. In the Quran, the family, not the individual woman, was the basic unit for which rights were defined. The woman was not responsible to earn her living or that of the family; since she was not expected to look after the family financially, it was only fair that the men, who had to look after the family financially, would get twice the women's share in inheritance, an argument again reminiscent of Fazlur Rahman. Furthermore, in a family where the wife got half her brother's share, the husband would get twice his own sister's share, which would mean that the family as a unit would have a share of inheritance similar to the one it would have had had women received an equal share (assuming the woman and the man come from families of similar wealth). A similar argument could be given regarding witnessing. Women who were not expected to earn their living outside the household would feel more comfortable pairing up with another woman in the public realm of the courtroom; unilateral divorce was not as easy as the secularists made it to be; similarly polygamy was allowed under certain exceptional circumstances which would be very difficult to fulfill in any case. G. S. could thus attribute a unity to Islam that was integral to her own defense of the religion.

Despite this defense of Islam as a fair and egalitarian system, which assumed the family not the individual as a unit of social rights, further on in the interview, G. S. presented her case for the importance of individual autonomy and self-realization. She explained how she believed women should work outside the home. She was an educated person, and it was difficult for an educated person to stay at home and realize herself and use all that she learned. She believed that women were victimized and had to make themselves accepted. Her earlier insistence on the sanctity and fairness of Islamic prescriptions for women had assumed a communal approach to rights, which would be realized within the family unit as a whole. She argued that, in Islam, even though a woman as an individual might not have as big a share of inheritance as her brother, the family she belonged would have a similar share to that of her brother's, which was ultimately fair. However, her later arguments reflected her regard for the woman as an individual with a need to prove herself within, as well as outside, her family. Both sets of moral frameworks coexisted and spurred her engagement with religiously inspired public life. She could assert herself and be the autonomous individual that she was in her engagement in Islamist politics. She did not make a problem of the apparently contradictory nature of the normative frameworks that shaped her life; she let them enrich one another.

Most women interviewed were more similar to A. N. than G. S. and much less concerned about what Islam had to say regarding women. Their knowledge of Islam or women in Islam was scant, but their faith was strong. They wanted to talk about the respect Islam accorded women, rather than the restrictions it entailed, which they believed seemed like restrictions only to the nonbelievers. They believed in God and Islam as ethically and morally impeccable, which meant that if polygamy was a decree, then there was a grand, sacred reason behind it. If polygamy was practiced in a way that hurt women, then Islam had not been correctly practiced. If men restricted women, then again it was because they did not know what Islam meant. For those influenced by feminist sensibilities, these were the patriarchal underpinnings of a social system that were mistakenly attributed to Islam. In a secular context in which there were no imminent implications of these laws for their personal lives, they could afford to think of Islam as the ideal system that they believed it to be. As Ç. H. argued, "I wish correct Islam could be practiced; I wish those countries practicing Islamic law practiced it properly. Our biggest problem is that there is no country that we could hold up as an example. Islam was practiced perfectly in its golden age, but since then we have been searching for the proper Islamic community as it should be. Of course, human beings are fallible. That is why there are the Quranic laws against wrongdoing. God has accepted from the beginning that human beings are prone to wrongdoing, but we have to study very hard to understand the correct Islam. Up till now only the squatter settlements and villages were pushed into Islam, rather than the educated urbanites. Well, whatever they could know of Islam—there was no studying and going back to the sources." Ç. H. was realistically aware that Islam had been ignored and delegitimized in the secular Republic, but she had faith that through learning, you could come up with a just and fair Islam that was reconcilable with what she believed: that Islam allowed for women's autonomy.

Some of those who had a stronger secular training and background thought that Quranic laws that could restrict women's rights were irrelevant to religious belief in this day and age. These women did not deny the existence of such dictates but believed that they could be bracketed. They argued that laicists exaggerated these dictates in order to denigrate Islam and what the Refah Party stood for. These women were closest to the statist Islam, which meant privatization of religion. They did not want to change the secular code in a fundamental way. Instead, they worked to enlarge the opportunity space where Islam could be practiced by individual believers but not the state.

Given the relative lack of power within the decision-making organs of the party, it was striking that these women had the faith their male leaders thought like they did and would continue to think alike regarding women's rights. Clearly women did not exhibit the strength to change a radically different perception male leaders could well have. The secular context in which they lived and the guarantees that the secular civil code provided made the issue of male prerogatives within Islam a non-issue. Their meaning and consequences were not real.

## HEADSCARF ISSUE

Refah women had diverse opinions on what Islamic dictates concerning women were, even though they all agreed that Islam was good for women. Some believed that Islam allowed for polygamy and that it was for the best (protecting widowed women); some elaborated that if polygamy hurt the women involved, then Islam was not being practiced properly. Others assumed polygamy was bad, but that in a practical sense you could not have polygamy in Islam because of all the religious restrictions on its practice. Despite this divergence of opinion concerning Islamic dictates, Welfare women unanimously insisted that the headscarf was a decree of God. They all agreed that female believers were obliged to cover their heads. Not all the women that we interviewed came to the party covered, even though for many of them the "ban on the headscarf" had been a crucial part of their process of engagement with the party. A couple of them covered after they worked in the party for some time. However, all the women interviewed were covered.

In our conversation, we suggested some of the arguments that could be made against the headscarf. Headscarves, it could be argued, constricted women physically and could be an encumbrance. They defined women primarily as a sexual being to the extent that they functioned to hide women's sexuality from the male gaze. Through the headscarf, women allowed their sexuality to be controlled. Imposition of the headscarf on women meant either that women were assumed to be too weak to protect themselves from aggressive male sexuality or that their sexuality was seen as threatening and too strong, such that there was a need to control it to protect society against their threat of disorder.

Refah women, in turn, gave the arguments commonly used in defense of the headscarf. They were not restricted by it physically. Mini skirts, rather than headscarves, emphasized women's sexuality and made them more vulnerable to sexual exploitation. Women were neither too weak nor too strong for wearing the headscarf. Adoption of the headscarf could not be explained with such simplistic terms as weakness or strength. Independent of what it could mean sociologically, the headscarf was a dictate of God and they wore it for the love of God, for religious reasons.

The headscarf issue was a sore one. It was also a most important one and ultimately the most immediate reason many women became engaged in the party. Those who traditionally covered their head saw the party as the sole defender of their worldviews. Those who covered later in life were victimized by the ban on the headscarf, because they had, for the most part, become professionals and then were prevented from practicing their professions. For this group, the party also became a vehicle that allowed them to realize their professional aspirations.

All the women had numerous stories of victimization because of the headscarf. Interestingly, most of the interviewees primarily resented that the ban on the headscarf obstructed the secular education of themselves or their children rather than their right to religious practice. Because the government practiced an understanding of Islam that prohibited head covering of students or civil servants, it prevented covered women from leading the kind of lives that the Republic, not necessarily their religion, expected them to lead. These women had internalized the norms of male-female equality in the public realm that the state upheld over the years, rather than the traditional role models that religion prescribed. Only a woman mentioned a link between education and religion to argue that Islam advised all believers to pursue education. She argued that believers were obstructed from practicing their religion regarding the pursuit of education. She reiterated the well-known saying attributed to the prophet Mohammed that people should go to China to study science if science developed in China. However, most others bracketed religious legitimation and elaborated on how they wanted to work and study but the ban obstructed them.

Women's sense of deprivation and victimization was ultimately because they wanted to practice religion the way they believed was correct at the same time as they lived the public lives they were used to. Defense of religious freedoms was inevitably at issue. E. S. bitterly claimed that with the ban on the headscarf the state was asking them to be either a citizen or a believer. In defending their right to practice their religion the way they believed was correct, many women referred to western models. These women might have pointed to the way things are in the West to convince the secularist pro-state constituency that looked up to the West, not because the West was a model they personally upheld. However despite this strategic choice, the reference nevertheless implied that how things are done in the West is a legitimate example for the women involved. N. E. complained, "This state looks up to the West in everything; they try to use the example of the West for anything. Why don't they look up to the West in this case? People are free to cover their heads in the West. Their states respect religious practice the way the believers choose to practice it. Even Clinton accepts that Muslims are okay the way they are." If Turkey wanted to be like the West, then it had to live up to the requirements of this choice. Ironically, N. E. attributed to the West an idealized liberalism that was not necessarily there, especially considering the headscarf bans in France and Germany. On the other hand, she would not consider the possibility that headscarves could be a sign of a fundamentalist threat challenging the liberalism she idealized.

Without exception, the women interviewed were frustrated because they did not understand why the state considered the headscarves a threat. A. N. protested, "Why is the state scared of half a meter of cloth? What can the wearing of the scarf do to the state?" A. N. thus tried to depolitize the headscarf and claim it to be merely an item of clothing. In contrast, N. K. tried to contextualize the issue within a normative realm: "What kind of morality is this such that obscenity and nudity is rampant in the press and the media whereas the covering of the hair is prohibited?" Implicit in N. K.'s question is the Islamist criticism of promiscuity and commodification of sexuality associated with western norms adopted by the secular Republic. Others claimed that those who opposed the headscarf were trite. A. S. said that there was reaction to the headscarf because the secularist found it unaesthetic: "If they find it unaesthetic then they should not look at it. The ones who are not covered claim the right to intervene in other people's head covers; have you ever seen anyone who is covered intervene in the outfit of anyone who is not covered?" While the claim might not have been true, as there were incidences of uncovered women being harassed in places where covered women were in the majority, this was the perception of a victim. A. S. thus was arguing that there were superficial reasons for opposition to the headscarf and that there was an unfair division of power regarding whose dress code would prevail.

Women interviewed were aware that the state prohibited the headscarves because it had become a political symbol. Many refused the claim. They insisted that they covered their head as a dictate of their religion and that it was a private concern. Z. S. retorted in protest, "Of course not. It is a private deal. How can they claim that it is political? What is the measure of the headscarf being political? How can they know it or measure it? Let them measure it if they will." Yet the political was difficult to disentangle from the private, especially according to Islam.

Religious codes dictated how to organize interpersonal relations and how to deal with marriage, inheritance, adultery, and divorce. The state had attempted to privatize religion and tried to sever the organic link Islam had to the political. The women interviewed, in their desire to expand the public space Islam could claim within the confines of the secular state, ignored the implications of their demands. They could afford to ignore the political nature of their Islamist demands, both because there was no imminent threat to their personal lives of an impending Islamic republic where laws could possibly change to reorganize their marriages and divorces and also because their own vision of Islam drew upon their experiences within the secular state. Their Islam was reconcilable with working outside the home, proving themselves in the public realm, and becoming the political citizens they could become. It did not entail the restrictions traditionally associated with Islam.

One interviewee denied the political nature of the headscarf and yet felt quite comfortable with the political implications of an Islamic state because it was idealized as a moral institution. R. D. explained, "Nothing like an Islamic state will come by just because we wear headscarves. Everyone is after his or her own interests. Those who oppose the party of religious people are scared that their interests will be undermined. If honest religious people come to power, the stealing and plundering will have to end. Those owners of big holding companies that do the stealing do not want it. What if a religious state comes? What if there is the Shariat? I don't care because I am an honest citizen who does not steal, who does not engage in adultery; I lead a moral life. Let the Shariat come; it is all right with me. People who are corrupt and can sustain their corrupt lives through this order are afraid of the Shariat. The important thing is democracy; let those who come be democratic." R. D. denied the political nature of the headscarf but was comfortable with the political implications of Islam. She was ready to endorse Islamic law, because she assumed it will hurt wrongdoers. Despite evidence to the contrary (Islamist businessmen have been charged with corruption and been involved in scandals), she believed that Islamists lead moral lives. Even though she had a very short-sighted, privatized understanding of Islam, she insisted on the importance of democracy. She would like to think of Islam as compatible with democracy, because democracy is a value that the secular system has instilled in her as important. She is ready to deny that Islam could allow for polygamy and unequal inheritance rights for women.

The women who deny the political nature of the headscarf and yet insist that it is a dictate of Islam are in a dilemma that they are not inclined to accept. Headscarves may be a dictate of Islam, but many Muslims claim that polygamy, unilateral divorce, and unequal inheritance rights are as well. After all, most Islamic countries allow for polygamy and these other dictates of the Shariat. They consider it to be part of Islamic law as much as the law concerning their headscarves. Are the women who insist on the headscarf ready to endorse other Islamic dictates? The interviewees unanimously refused the analogy. If such groups prevailed, they had the determination to have their "true Islam" reign. They were not ready to live with these other dictates concerning women that were practiced in many Muslim states.

In the Refah Party top-level decision-making organs, women were denied sharing power with men. As women who had experience of this denial, one would expect that the respondents would be more concerned about a monopoly of power by Muslim men. The party leaders did not ask women's opinions on how to run the party, and if they came to power there was no reason to expect that these men would ask women's opinions on how to run the country. Auspiciously, the women claimed a determination to work for the kind of Islam they believed in.

The women with the headscarves who belittled the threat of Islamic fundamentalism insisted on their own version of Islam that was ultimately based on a unique Turkish experience. They did not understand why they could be seen as a threat to the secular state, because their understanding of Islam was shaped with the values and norms of this secular state. They respect the secular or liberal concepts of justice and fairness. Considering the responses of the interviewees in light of the headscarf issue in Turkey, for the majority the political nature of their headscarves did not mean that they were opposed to a secular democratic Republic that upheld respect for the individual. Women who covered their heads and worked for the party wanted to operate within the framework of a secular Republic where religion was allowed to be more publicly visible. Even those few women who would prefer to see an Islamic republic preferred to see one that was substantively similar to the secular Republic they knew.[15] Their view of the Islamic republic was shaped by what they knew, namely a republic where women had similar legal opportunities to men. They wanted the headscarves but not polygamy. Even when they claimed polygamy was an Islamic dictate, they also claimed that it could not be practically practiced or that it could be restrained. They wanted an Islamic state because they associated it with a moral secular state.

While these women might not be an imminent threat to the secular order, it is clear that the secular order, with its tools of secular education, has been quite inept in teaching its citizens the probable implications of an appeal to religion in legitimizing the state. The interviewees shaped their Islam on secular models, but they did not realize that ultimately there was a radical difference between a state that appealed to its constituency for legitimation and one that sought legitimation with a reference to a sacred God that could not be criticized, transformed, or argued with. Anyone who claimed to rule in the name of God to dispense his justice could easily manipulate his power because of the sacred, hence unreachable, source of legitimacy he claimed.

Yet, to enhance the parameters of democratic participation, and in light of the interviews, we need to recognize that the meaning of political symbolism that the state attributed to headscarved women is radically different than the one these women themselves have. If the main concern of the state in banning the headscarves is a threat to its liberal democracy, then under conditions where the Islamist women ultimately endorse the liberal secular values of the regime, such a threat is minimal. It can be accommodated by a liberal democracy, especially if the Islamist women are more clear about the boundaries within which they want to practice Islam and the state is respectful of their own definitions of what they mean with their headscarves.

# Conclusion

Clifford Geertz has argued, "The development of liberalism with both the courage and the capacity to engage itself with a different world, one in which its principles are neither well understood nor widely held, in which indeed it is, in most places, a minority creed, alien and suspect, is not only possible, it is necessary."[1] The "development of liberalism" in Turkey where liberal "principles are neither well understood nor widely held" has followed a circuitous road. Since its inception, the Turkish republic has never been a liberal haven, but liberalism has pushed its way nevertheless. The stories of Refah women tell us why the development of liberalism in a Muslim context is not only possible but also necessary. It can enrich democracy as well as liberalism. This final chapter retraces the implications of the experiences of Refah women for liberalism and democracy by focusing on secularism and women in Turkey.

## REPUBLICAN STATE AND ITS SECULARISM

The successes of women in the commissions had implications for the strengths and weaknesses of secularism in Turkey. Islamist female activists challenged the hubris of the secular state and those citizens who endorse its principles of secularism. Under the circumstances of the 1920s, when the modernizing political elites introduced the concept and practice of secularism in a Muslim context, they not only separated religion from politics but also put it under state control. This understanding of secularism ignored the restrictions secularism posed on religious freedoms. The state, which tried to privatize religion, defined how much visibility Islam could have in public life, how it could be taught, who could teach it, and how it could be interpreted. By the 1980s, the Islamists in general and Refah women in particular questioned that secularism need be defined in the restrictive manner that the state did.

109

Women's challenge was critical. The Republic had cultivated its revolutionary secularism with women. It was long assumed that women benefited most from Republican secularism. Hence, women's turning into Islam was a most unexpected challenge, a betrayal for the staunch secularists. The Refah women waged an organized battle against the state, which banned headscarves in universities. They questioned the meaning and intentions that the state attributed to those who want to wear headscarves. They contested that the state can maintain its understanding of secularism by repressing university students' demands to wear headscarves and restricting the parameters of politics by ostracizing women using Islamist language to oppose state policies. Refah women's engagement in politics exposed the limits to which the secular reforms delivered civil liberties.

Even though the modernizing reforms of the Republican state were successful in institutionalizing secularism and expanding the socio-economic and political opportunities of a steadily growing population, they had their limits. The education provided by the state could not lure large numbers of people, including women who perhaps benefited most from the secularizing reforms, into its particular secularism. The state was unsuccessful in reaching this group who opted to seek guidance in life through Islam. Consequently, women who endorsed a different reading of Islam were almost disfranchised. Unable to shape or integrate women who had an alternate understanding of Islam, the state, instead, chose to punish them by excluding them from joining its institutions. The Islamist female activists thus pointed not merely to the inability of the state to perpetuate its ideology but also to the state's attempt to silence those who challenged it. When the women were ostracized from public education and public office, they turned their energies to work for a party that would support their self-identity.

The experiences of Refah women did not merely point to the weakness of the state in cultivating an accommodating secularism but also testified to its success in permeating society with its secular values. The Islamist women endorsed a unique Islam shaped by the principles and practices of the secular society in which they lived. Ironically, the Islam these women upheld was not the threatening Islam that the state attributed to them. An Islamic conception of equality that prioritizes complementarity between the sexes, thereby justifying polygamy or discrepancies in inheritance rights, can be a threat to liberal values that claim formal equality between the sexes. Yet, the Islamist women interviewed either compartmentalized the blatantly illiberal aspects of their religion and contained them or reinterpreted them to adjust to their liberal convictions. They belonged to two worlds that liberalized their religious proclivities at the same time as it challenged a narrow understanding of secularism.

The context in which these Islamist women were socialized was important in shaping their religious convictions. The Republic provided these women with the kind of education that expanded their capabilities and gave them the skills they could use in their particular political mission. These women could engage in the work they did, because the Republic legitimized democratic pursuit of political interests for men as well as women. To the extent that the Republic paid homage to universal human rights, which included respect for the individual and political liberalism, the women of the commissions ultimately shared its values. They were conscious to reject an Islam that was incompatible with these liberal dictates, one that could impede their growth as individuals. Through their work within the commissions, they could develop themselves and  their political skills, including speaking, persuasion, and negotiation, as individuals. They could improve their feelings of political efficacy as they witnessed the success of their labor.[2]

Feminist Myra Jehlen argued, "There are many ways of dealing with contradictions . . . of which only one is to try to resolve them. Another way amounts to joining a contradiction—engaging it not so much for the purpose of overcoming it as to tap its energy."[3] Female activists inspired by a religious ideology and brought up in a secular world "engaged" in the contradiction of these two seemingly antithetical paradigms of their lives "to tap in its energy." Their secular drives to prove themselves to themselves led them to justify and defend their political activism in the public realm with reference to secular norms, such as individual rights. They lived Islam to define their identities as they chose to define it. Their Islam was neither the Islam of the secular state nor that of the traditional Muslim patriarchs who restricted women's rights. Despite a staunch defense of their particular understandings of Islam, which were mostly defined with reference to their experience of secular laws that guaranteed equal rights to women, their "Islams" varied immensely and were not monolithic. The story of the Refah activists shows that the experience of Islam is contextual as well as individualistic. In a secular context, secular values permeate the experience of the devout and shape the way they live Islam. The potential threat of authoritarianism in a turn to a unitary, fundamentalist Islam is not at issue when people who practice the religion interpret it as a dynamic ideology compatible with their secular, individualistic lifestyles.

The Turkish case shows that in a secular context, however limited that secularism might have been, liberal norms infiltrated those comprehensive religious views and shaped them such that believers respected the individualistic norms liberal democracies cultivated. If we want to expand democratic boundaries consistent with the dictates of liberal rights, preconceived notions of what Islam is need to be overcome, because those who practice it might not pose the problems that we attribute to them. In practice there might be more of an interchange, transgression and influence between seemingly irreconcilable worldviews such as Islam and liberal democracy. As Martha Nussbaum argues, "What counts as Jewish, or Muslim, or Christian is not in any simple way read off from the past. Although traditions vary in the degree and nature of their dynamism, they are defined at least in some ways by where their members want to go."[4]

## WOMEN AND POLITICAL PARTICIPATION

The challenge of the Islamist women had implications for women at large and their political participation. To the extent that women's political participation is a dictate of democracy, women of the commissions enlarged the boundaries of democratic participation. They helped integrate not merely those who contested Republican secularism in the name of a more publicly visible Islam but also those who were assumed to be disinterested in politics because of their gender. Some of the prejudices concerning women were recast. The experience of the women in the commissions challenged the assumption that women are not interested in active party politics in Turkey, that they cannot make a difference in politics, and that there is a public and private divide that excludes women and defines where politics can take place. The women of the commissions realized that those captive in the private realm, the housewives, were eager and ready to move to the political realm. The commissions, which had their largest successes in large metropolitan centers, carried out their activities primarily among migrant housewives from rural backgrounds. In the familiar milieu of their own or their neighbor's houses where housewives felt most comfortable, the ladies' commissions approached women who had been unable to have their voices carried to the political realm and showed that these women could be in politics.

The nature of the way women moved into politics was a radical critique of the political process that alienated half the population. It exposed the fact that political parties needed to give more serious attention to women who are ready to be politicized in pursuit of their self-interests. Housewives could not be moved into the public realm with exhortations of a good life imposed from above. Rather, they did so when party members attended to the interests and concerns of these women defined by the women themselves and promised to make them heard in the political domain.

In this process, Republican modernism that defined itself in opposition to tradition was also challenged. The women of the commissions crossed the boundaries between the traditional and the modern when they carried political interests that were captive in the private realm into politics. They endowed traditional networks and communal modes of social interaction such as reception days (*kabul günleri*) and home visits with a new political ethos to reach their constituency. Both the religious discourse that inspired the activists and the neighborhood networks they benefited from upheld communal values. The traditional communal values that sustained bonds of neighborhood networks, and which the women of the commissions benefited from, critically sustained the individual empowerment of both the female activists and the constituency of women that came out onto the political scene as individuals. These women could thus have a sense of themselves as individuals. The boundaries between the traditional and the modern became blurred when the traditional values of "communalism" sustained the modern, liberal values of "individualism." There was no simple dichotomy between that which was traditional and that which was modern. The Islamist women who were stigmatized as promoting traditional values and ways of life were in fact reconfiguring the modernist paradigm to make it their own. They succeeded in recruiting the women not with an appeal to a religious ideology but rather with an appeal to the interests of the people involved. To expand the parameters of democratic participation in modernizing contexts, they proved that traditions could assume new roles. Crossing the boundaries between modern electoral politics and traditional community networks was instrumental in facilitating inclusion of excluded groups into the democratic process.

## LIBERAL DEMOCRACY AND ISLAM

The experiences of Refah women show us that liberalism and Islam need not be mutually exclusive. In the context of Turkish secularism, liberalism infiltrated Islam, at least partially, in the way some women lived Islam. Entry of Islam into political life was not, in the words of Clifford Geertz, "pathological—primitive, backward, regressive and irrational."[5] To the contrary, it expanded the reach of liberalism and deepened its practice even when it only partially shaped the lives of women who lived Islam through politics.

Refah women were a heterogeneous group. Many of them made deliberate, uncoerced choices in deciding to lead a more religious life than their cohorts, covering their hair and working for the party. They chose their marriage partners themselves, at times against the wishes of their families. These were autonomous choices upheld by liberal proclivities. Yet we could not generalize these experiences. Some women were simply born into more religious families in which their parents helped them choose their husbands, but these women nevertheless made independent, autonomous decisions working for the party.

Even those women who had made the radical choice of moving from more secular to more religious lives practiced liberal as well as non-liberal norms. Most of these women abided by Islamist teachings regarding division of labor within the family not that different from what most secular women experienced. Yet Islamist women made sure that these Islamic or traditional sex roles they subscribed to did not interfere with their active and autonomous public roles. They advocated that maternal duties to children and obedience to husbands were priorities for Islam and for themselves, but they made sure, whether or not they were conscious of the process, that these priorities did not obstruct their political commitments where liberal principles of self-creation and autonomy prevailed. However, there were also cases where women enhanced their autonomy at home and became more independent of their husbands when they became successful political actors in the public realm. Liberal proclivities gradually spread over the private realm, particularly when women proved their autonomy in the public realm.

Non-liberal practices were not restricted to the private realm. Glass ceilings prevented women from assuming positions of power within the party's decision-making organs. Even though women themselves might have run the commissions democratically, as they insisted they did, there was no internal democracy within the party, which was run hierarchically. Neither of these non-liberal practices was unique to Refah. So-called secular parties were similarly guilty of both glass ceilings for women and hierarchic practices. Yet, in a pro-Islamic party the likelihood of an appeal to an exclusionary, patriarchal Islam is like a sword of Democles that looms over the liberal ethos Islamist women share. One could further surmise that the democracy women insisted they had within the ladies' commissions was limited, because the Islamist ideological solidarity possibly dampened internal dissent. Even though Islamist move into politics might not have been primitive or reactionary, it was no beacon of liberalism either.

Yet there was cross-fertilization; as Islam moved into politics, liberal values penetrated Islam. There were areas where liberal practices prevailed and others where communal norms legitimized by Islam did. Just as a comprehensive Islam did not define the lives of these women, an exclusive liberalism did not hold its sway either. There was cultural contestation and influence. Islam seemed to be changing from within by women who practiced it.

If we believe, along with contemporary liberal theorists,[6] that culture is important for the individual whether because it provides the context of choice and autonomy or because it fosters a communal identity, then a richer liberal democracy might have to accommodate an Islamic worldview that is engaged in a dynamic relationship with liberal values. Using a criterion such as Will Kymlicka's "internal restrictions"—whereby groups that seek protection have to make sure not to restrict the civil rights of their members—might be inappropriate to judge if this group is fit to be protected in a liberal democracy. In a heterogeneous group some members might be exposed to internal restrictions but not others, assuming all parties accept what is meant by an "internal restriction" and consider that it is a bad thing. Moreover, people and their practices change over time. Refah women were neither a homogenous nor a static group. Some of the women were exposed to what we could call internal restrictions in some and not other aspects of their lives. The women themselves might not have agreed. Over time, even these disputed restrictions were not practiced; others remained. It was possible for liberalism to expand its sway and influence many Islamist women, which has in turn enriched both liberalism as well as Islam.

Refah women did not precipitate a liberal or feminist protest within their conservative Islamist party.[7] Neither did they succeed in promoting female activists or supporters to positions of power within the party hierarchy. Yet, with their autonomous choices, they did challenge the parameters within which women were expected to practice Islam, to engage in politics, and to promote their self-interest in Turkey. They situated themselves at the crossroads of women's political participation and Turkish political history to contest statist principles of secularism and western modernization. They expanded opportunities of self-expression for themselves as well as for other women who were deemed apathetic to politics. In a country where communitarian values have traditionally prevailed, they introduced a rival notion of a communitarian common good to the state's and they tested the democratic contentions of the state. Bhikhu Parekh claims that "it is the glory of liberal (that is, tolerant, open and free) society that it is not, and does not need or even seek to become, exclusively or entirely liberal (that is, committed to a strong sense of autonomy, individualism, self-creation, and so on)."[8] Refah women could have belonged to such a society. They did not. Instead, they taught us about a cultural dialogue that could enrich liberalism as well as Islam and make democracy more inclusive.

# Appendix:
# Questions Used in the Interviews

## PERSONAL QUESTIONS

- Could you tell me about yourself?
- Where were you born?
- Who were your parents?
- What were their occupations?
- Which schools did you attend?
- Are you married?
- What is your husband's profession?
- When and how did you develop your interest in Islam?
- Did a friend, a certain group of people, or other factors evoke your interest in Islam?
- When did you become involved with the Refah Party?
- Did some people, the party's ideology, or institutions affect your decision to work for the party?
- Why did you begin working for the party?
- Did you like working for the party? Why?
- Who educated you in the party?
- How were you educated in the party?

## ORGANIZATION OF THE LADIES COMMISSIONS

- Could you tell me about the organization of the ladies' commissions?
- How many provinces did you have branches in?
- What units were important in the organization?

- How were these units linked to one another?
- Would you receive criticism from the upper ranks of the party hierarchy?
- How frequently did you get criticism? On what issues?
- How did you respond to this criticism? Did you promptly utilize it or react to it?
- How autonomous from or dependent on the Central Party Organs were the Ladies' Commissions?
- Which decisions or what issues did the central organs shape?
- Do you have any background information about the founding of the ladies' commissions?
- How far did the political cleavages within the Refah Party get reflected to the ladies commissions?
- Who decided on the agenda or the division of labor within the ladies' commissions?
- Did you have relations with other Islamist organizations or groups? At what level and with what frequency were these relations carried out?

## ACTIVITIES

- What activities did you engage in as an organization?
- How did you carry out these activities?
- What subjects were introduced in the home visits or private gatherings? What did you tell these people you visited?
- Were there differences between commissions organized in different provinces or districts? What were these differences?
- We hear about the widespread use of modern technology within the Refah Party organization; for example, computers, videos. Did you use these? What were the video shows about?
- What were the topics you introduced in your public relations activities with public institutions such as hospitals or unions?
- Could you give us some information about your educational programs? What subjects did they cover?
- Who attended these programs?
- Who helped you in your educational programs?
- What did you teach the party functionaries?

- How did the female activists find the time to engage in these activities?
- How could you be so successful in extending your organization in such a short time?
- What do you think were the factors or circumstances which made you successful?

## MEMBERS

- How many members did you have in the particular organization you worked for (at the province or the district level)?
- Did all the members pay their dues?
- In what provinces or districts were you more successful in recruiting new members? What do you think were the reasons?
- Who were your members (housewives/old people/young people/ wives of Refah men)? Did they follow Islamist publications or television? Did you introduce them to the Islamist media? What were some regional differences in membership?
- Were your members headscarved? Did they cover their heads after they became members of the Refah Party, or were they already headscarved before they joined the party?
- How did you convince women who were not interested in the Refah Party to become members?
- Why do you think women became members of the party?
- Were the women who became members usually those whose husbands already favored the Refah Party?
- Did women get permission or inform their husbands when they registered with the party?
- Did the husbands approve, disapprove, encourage, or discourage their wives when the latter wanted to become members of the Refah Party?
- Were there problems when the husbands of the women you registered did not approve of the party or the membership of their wives?

  Do you think there were women who influenced their husbands to become members of the party or vote for it?
- How would you evaluate the efficacy or the usefulness of the ladies' commissions for the party in general?

## VIEWS

- Do you think you live as a good Muslim should? (Do you follow the requirements of Islam, such as five daily prayers and fasting, etc.?)
- Do you think you can give a Muslim identity to your children?
- How did your work with the party affect your children?
- It has been argued that Islamic rules regarding marriage, divorce, inheritance, and witnessing in court are biased in favor of men, that is, inegalitarian. What do you think on this issue?
- It is argued that Islam promotes the traditional division of labor between men and women. What do you think on this issue?
- Do you think the Refah Party reflected an Islamist position on women's issues?
- Claims are made that headscarves are a control mechanism over women and their sexuality. What do you think about this claim or about women covering their heads?
- What do you think about women's electoral rights, especially for being elected to office?
- What do you think about violence toward women?
- What do you think about the traditional division of labor between men and women, particularly as it pertains to women? Should women work outside the home?
- What do you think the Republican reforms brought to Turkey? Could certain reforms be carried out differently? What do you see as the strengths and weaknesses of these reforms?

# Notes

## INTRODUCTION

1. The study resulted in the report, Yeşim Arat, *Political Islam in Turkey and Women's Organizations, Istanbul, TESEV, 1999*. By the term "Islamist," I refer to Islam as a political ideology rather than a private religious belief. In practice, this is defined loosely by different groups of people who argue for expanding the public space Islam has in the Turkish context. The term is vague, as it covers a wide range of positions and people with contradictory beliefs about what the role of Islam should be in public life, but helpful to draw attention to the difference between the traditional Muslim population who has reached a modus vivendi with the secular state and those who contest state control over Islam.

2. The court maintained that the party undermined principles of secularism established in the constitution.

3. Clifford Geertz, *Interpretation of Cultures*, New York, Basic Books, 1973, p. 22.

4. Charles Taylor et al., *Multiculturalism*, Princeton, N.J., Princeton University Press, 1994; Will Kymlicka, *Multicultural Citizenship: A Liberal Theory of Minority Rights*, Oxford, Clarendon Press, 1995, *Politics in the Vernacular: Nationalism, Multiculturalism and Citizenship*, Oxford, New York, Oxford University Press, 2001, Will Kymlicka and Wayne Norman (eds.), *Citizenship in Diverse Societies*, Oxford, New York, Oxford University Press, 2000; Susan Okin et al., *Is Multiculturalism Bad for Women*, Princeton, N.J., Princeton University Press, 1999; Bhikhu Parekh, *Rethinking Multiculturalism: Cultural Diversity and Political Theory*, Cambridge, Mass., Harvard University Press, 2002 (second printing); Seyla Benhabib, *The Claims of Culture*, Princeton and Oxford, Princeton University Press, 2002.

5. Joseph Raz, *The Morality of Freedom*, Oxford, Clarendon Press, 1986; Will Kymlicka, *Multicultural Citizenship: A Liberal Theory of Minority Rights*, Oxford, Clarendon Press, 1995; Will Kymlicka, *Politics in the Vernacular: Nationalism, Multiculturalism and Citizenship*, Oxford, New York, Oxford University Press, 2001.

6. Samuel Huntington, *The Clash of Civilizations and the Remaking of World Order*, New York, Simon and Schuster, 1996.

7. Cited in Seyla Benhabib, "Unholy Politics," *Constellations: An International Journal of Critical and Democratic Theory*, March 2002, pp. 34–45.

8. Niyazi Berkes, *The Development of Secularism in Turkey*, Montreal, McGill University Press, 1964; Binnaz Toprak, *Islam and Political Development in Turkey*, Leiden, E. J. Brill, 1981.

9. Bernard Lewis, *The Emergence of Modern Turkey*, London, Oxford University Press, 1976 (third printing); Metin Heper, *The State Tradition in Turkey*, Walkington, Eothen, 1985; Çağlar Keyder, *State and Class in Turkey*, London, Verso, 1987; Feroz Ahmad, *The Making of Modern Turkey*, London, Routledge, 1993.

10. Binnaz Toprak, *Islam and Political Development in Turkey*; Andrew Davison, *Secularism and Revivalism in Turkey*, New Haven, Conn., Yale University Press, 1998.

11. Bernard Lewis, *The Emergence of Modern Turkey*, p. 416.

12. Haldun Gülalp, "The Poverty of Democracy in Turkey: The Refah Party Episode," *New Perspectives on Turkey*, Fall, no. 21, 1999, pp. 38–40.

13. For a rich anthropological description of the hostility between the two groups, particularly the secularist fear of the Islamists, see Yael Navaro-Yashin, *Faces of the State*, Princeton, N.J., Princeton University Press, 2002, Chapter 1.

14. Metin Heper, *The State Tradition in Turkey*.

15. Şerif Mardin, *Jön Türklerin Siyasi Fikirleri* (Political Thoughts of the Young Turks), İstanbul, İletişim Yayınları, 1983, p. 223.

16. Feroz Ahmad, "The Progressive Republican Party, 1923–1945" in Metin Heper and Jacob Landau (eds.), *Political Parties and Democracy in Turkey*, London, I.B.Tauris, 1991, pp. 65–82.

17. On the relationship of women and the Republic, see Yeşim Arat, "The Project of Modernity and Women in Turkey," in Sibel Bozdoğan and Reşat Kasaba, *Rethinking Modernity and National Identity in Turkey*, Seattle, University of Washington Press, 1997, pp. 95–112; on the meaning of Islamist dress in Turkish socio-political transformation, see Nilüfer Göle, *The Forbidden Modern: Civilization and Veiling*, Ann Arbor, The University of Michigan Press, 1996; for the claim that a most significant characteristic of Islamic culture is its outlook on women and sex, see Yılmaz Esmer, "Is There an Islamic Civilization" in Ronald Inglehart (ed.), *Human Values and Social Change*, Leiden, E. J. Brill, 2003, pp. 35–68.

18. Ruşen Çakır, *Ne Şeriat Ne Demokrasi* (Neither Shariat Nor Democracy), İstanbul, Metis Yayınları, 1994, p. 244.

19. *Cumhuriyet*, February 17, 1994.

20. *Milliyet*, December 29, 1993.

21. *Milli Gazete*, February 16, 1994.

22. *Hürriyet*, March 30, 1994.

23. *Yeni Yüzyıl*, September 25, 1998.

24. On the role of religion in Turkish politics, see Şerif Mardin, "Religion and Secularism in Turkey" in Ali Kazancıgil and E. Özbudun (eds.), *Atatürk: Founder of a Modern State*, London, C. Hirst, 1981, pp. 191–219, *Religion and Social Change in Modern Turkey*, Albany, State University of New York

Press, 1989; Binnaz Toprak, "Politicization of Islam in a Secular State: The National Salvation Party in Turkey," in Said Amir Arjomand (ed.), *From Nationalism to Revolutionary Islam*, Albany, State University of New York Press, 1984, pp. 119–33, "Surviving Modernization: Islam as Communal Means of Adaptation," *Il Politico*, 56, 1991, pp. 147–61, "Islam and the Secular State in Turkey," in Çiğdem Balım et al. (eds.), *Turkey: Political, Social and Economic Challenges in the 1990s*, Leiden, E. J. Brill, 1995, pp. 90–96; Faruk Birtek and Binnaz Toprak, "The Conflictual Agendas of Neo-Liberal Reconstruction and the Rise of Islamic Politics in Turkey: The Hazards of Rewriting Modernity," *Praxis International*, July 1993, pp. 192–212; Ali Yaşar Sarıbay, *Türkiye'de Modernleşme Din ve Parti Politikası: MSP Örnek Olayı* (Modernization, Religion and Party Politics in Turkey: The NSP Case), İstanbul, Alan Yayıncılık, 1985; Metin Heper, "Islam and Democracy in Turkey: Toward a Reconciliation," *Middle East Journal*, 51/1, 1997, pp. 32–45; Ümit Cizre Sakallıoğlu, "Parameters and Strategies of Islam—State Interaction in Republican Turkey," *International Journal of Middle Eastern Studies*, 28, 1996, pp. 231–51; İlter Turan, "Religion and Political Culture in Turkey," in R. L. Tapper (ed.), *Islam in Modern Turkey: Religion, Politics and Literature in a Secular State*, London, I.B.Tauris, 1991 pp. 31–55; on the importance of religious elites in Turkey, Nilüfer Göle, "Secularism and Islamism in Turkey: The Making of Elites and Counter-Elites," *Middle East Journal*, 51/1, 1997, pp. 46–58; on the emergence and significance of the Refah Party in Turkish politics, Hakan Yavuz, "Political Islam and the Welfare (Refah) Party in Turkey," *Comparative Politics*, 30/1, 1997, pp. 63–82; Haldun Gülalp, "A Postmodern Reaction to Dependent Modernization: The Social and Historical Roots of Islamic Radicalism," *New Perspectives on Turkey*, Fall, 8, 1992, pp. 15–26, "Political Islam in Turkey: The Rise and Fall of the Refah Party," *Muslim World*, January, vol. LXXXIX, no. 1, 1999, pp. 22–41, "The Poverty of Democracy in Turkey: The Refah Party Episode," *New Perspectives on Turkey*, Fall, no. 21, 1999b, pp. 35–60; Jenny B. White, "Pragmatists or Ideologues? Turkey's Welfare Party in Power," *Current History*, 1997, pp. 25–30, "The Islamist Paradox" in Deniz Kandiyoti and Ayşe Saktanber (eds.), *Fragments of Culture: The Everyday of Modern Turkey*, London, New York, I.B.Tauris, 2002, pp. 191–217; on an anthropological study of Refah Party-led political mobilization, see Jenny B. White, *Islamist Mobilization in Turkey: A Study in Vernacular Politics*, Seattle, University of Washington Press, 2002; on women living Islam, Ayşe Saktanber, *Living Islam: Women, Religion and the Politicization of Culture in Turkey*, London, I.B.Tauris, 2002; on Islamist women's civil society organizations, Barbara Pusch, "Stepping into the Public Sphere: The Rise of Islamist and Religious Conservative Women's Non-Governmental Organizations" in Stefanos Yerasimos et al. (eds.), *Civil Society in the Grip of Nationalism*, Istanbul, Orient Institute, 2000, pp. 475–505.

25. Nevval Sevindi, August 26–30, October 12, 15, 1996, *Yeni Yüzyıl*.

26. Susan Carroll and Linda Zerilli, "Feminist Challenges to Political Science" in Ada Finifer (ed.), *Political Science: The State of the Discipline I*, Washington, D.C., The American Political Science Association, 1993, pp. 55–76.

27. The Fazilet Party was also closed down by a Constitutional Court decision in the summer of 2001. The court claimed that the Fazilet Party was

a continuation of the Refah Party and similarly became the locus of anti-secular religious activism. Two prominent female members of the Fazilet Party were banned from politics because of their activities in support of the Islamist headscarves, which the Constitutional Court judged as a symbol of opposition to the secular republic and a threat to its stability. After the Fazilet Party was closed, the Islamists split. Adalet ve Kalkınma (Justice and Development) Party, founded by a younger generation of so-called reformist leaders, came to power in the November 3, 2002 elections with 34 percent of the vote. On the developments following the Refah Party's demise, see Ziya Öniş, "Political Islam at the Crossroads: From Hegemony to Co-existence," *Contemporary Politics*, vol. 7, no. 4, 2001, pp. 281–98. On the nature of military pressure, which precipitated the closing of the Refah Party, see Jeremy Salt, "Turkey's Military 'Democracy' " *Current History*, 1999, pp. 72–78.

28. Welfare Party documents and brochures were gathered through party members, colleagues, and students who had acquired them before the party was closed.

29. Alev Çınar, "Refah Party and the City Administration of Istanbul: Liberal Islam, Localism and Hybridity," *New Perspectives on Turkey*, Spring, 16, 1997, pp. 23–40.

## 1. WOMEN OF THE REPUBLIC AND ISLAM

1. Andrew Davison, *Secularism and Revivalism in Turkey*, New Haven, Conn., Yale University Press, 1998, pp. 197–98.

2. Ziya Gökalp, *Türkçülüğün Esasları* (Principles of Turkism), İstanbul, Varlık Yayınları, 1968) pp. 147–48. On nationalism and women in Turkey, see Deniz Kandiyoti, "Women and the Turkish State: Political Actors or Symbolic Pawns?" in Nira Yuval-Davis and Floya Anthias (eds.), *Women–Nation–State*, London, The Macmillan Press, 1989, pp. 126–49, "Identity and Its Discontents: Women and the Nation," *Millennium: Journal of International Studies*, 20, 3, 1991, pp. 429–43.

3. Afet İnan, *Atatürk Hakkında Hatıralar ve Belgeler* (Documents and Memories on Atatürk), Ankara, Türk Tarih Kurumu Basımevi, 1959, p. 257.

4. Serpil Çakır, *Osmanlı Kadın Hareketi* (Ottoman Women's Movement), İstanbul, Metis Yayınları, 1993.

5. Zafer Toprak, "1935 İstanbul Uluslararası Feminizm Kongresi ve Barış" (The 1935 International Istanbul Feminism Congress and Peace), *Toplum-Düşün*, March 1986, no. 24, pp. 24–29; Yaprak Zihnioğlu, *Kadınsız İnkılap* (Revolution Without Women), İstanbul, Metis Yayınları, 2003.

6. Quoted in Ayşe Durakbaşa, "Cumhuriyet Döneminde Kemalist Kadın Kimliğinin Oluşumu" (The Formation of Kemalist Woman's Identity in the Republican Period), *Tarih ve Toplum*, March 1988, 51, p. 43.

7. Yeşim Arat, "The Project of Modernity and Women in Turkey" in Sibel Bozdoğan and Reşat Kasaba (eds.), *Rethinking Modernity and National Identity in Turkey*, Seattle, University of Washington Press, 1997, p. 101.

8. Zehra Arat argues that the republic was engaged in the "reconstruction of traditional society within a new, nationalist context." See Zehra Arat,

"Turkish Women and the Republican Reconstruction of Tradition" in Fatma Müge Göçek and Shiva Balaghi (eds.), *Reconstructing Gender in the Middle East,* New York, Columbia University Press, 1994, p. 59. She further argues that the "major accomplishment of civil law was the establishment of state control over the institution of family" (p. 63). Even though this might be a harsh judgment regarding the Republican reforms, traditional forms of patriarchy did continue in different forms while women were given the opportunities to educate themselves and to fight those norms in due time.

9. Yael Navaro, " 'Using the Mind' at Home: The Rationalization of Housewifery in Early Republican Turkey (1928–1940)," honors thesis submitted to the Department of Sociology, Brandeis University, 1991.

10. Labor force participation rate of women was 34 percent in Turkey nationwide and 17 percent in urban areas of Turkey, according to 1999 statistics taken after 1998 when the Refah Party was closed; see *Women in Turkey,* General Directorate on the Status and Problems of Women, 1999, Ankara, no author. The percentages were not much different in previous decades. Most of the women employed outside the urban labor force were unpaid agricultural laborers.

11. Ayse Öncü, "Turkish Women in the Professions: Why So Many?" in Nermin Abadan Unat (ed.), *Women in Turkish Society,* Leiden, E. J. Brill, 1981, pp. 180–93.

12. Feride Acar, "Turkish Women in Academia: Roles and Careers," *METU Studies in Development,* 10, 1983, pp. 409–46.

13. Nermin Abadan-Unat, "Social Change and Turkish Women" in N. Abadan Unat (ed.), *Women in Turkish Society,* Leiden, E. J. Brill, 1981, p. 5.

14. Yeşim Arat, *Patriarchal Paradox: Women Politicians in Turkey,* Madison, N.J., Fairleigh Dickinson University Press, 1989.

15. Nükhet Sirman, "Feminism in Turkey: A Short History," *New Perspectives on Turkey,* 3, 1989, pp. 1–34.

16. Şirin Tekeli, "Emergence of the Feminist Movement in Turkey," in Drude Dahlerup (ed.), *The New Women's Movement: Feminism and Political Power in Europe and the USA,* London, Sage Publications, 1986, pp. 179–99.

17. Şirin Tekeli, "Women in the Changing Political Associations of the 1980s," in Andrew Finkel and Nükhet Sirman (eds.), *Turkish State, Turkish Society,* London, Routledge, 1990, pp. 259–88.

18. Ayşe Öncü, "The Interaction of Politics, Religion and Finance: Islamic Banking in Turkey," paper presented at the Symposium on Muslims, Migrants and Metropolis, Berlin Institute for Comparative Social Research, Berlin, 1989; Ayşe Buğra, "Class, Culture and State: An Analysis of Two Turkish Business Associations," *International Journal of Middle Eastern Studies,* November 1998, pp. 521–39.

19. Ruşen Çakır, *Direniş ve İtaat: İki İktidar Arasında İslamcı Kadın* (Resistance and Obedience: Islamist Woman Between Two Authorities), İstanbul, Metis Yayınları, 2000.

20. Cihan Aktaş, *Kadının Serüveni* (Adventure of Woman), İstanbul, Girişim Yayıncılık, 1986, p. 211.

21. Ibid, p. 212.

22. For Islamist women's perception of secular and/or feminist women, see Yıldız Ramazanoğlu, "Yol Ayrımında İslamcı ve Feminist Kadınlar" (Islamist and Feminist Women at the Crossroads) in Yıldız Ramazanoğlu (ed.), *Osmanlı'dan Cumhuriyet'e Kadının Tarihi Dönüşümü* (The Historical Transformation of Woman from Ottoman Times to the Republic), İstanbul, Pınar Yayınları, 2000, pp. 139–67; Halise Çiftçi "Bizim feministlerden değil, onların bizden alacakları çok şey var" (There is a lot feminists can take from us, not us from them), *Milli Gazete*, February 16, 1996.

23. Cihan Aktaş, *Kadının Serüveni*, p. 211.

24. Ruşen Çakır, *Direniş ve İtaat: İki İktidar Arasında İslamcı Kadın*, p. 130.

25. Ibid, pp. 45–56; Sibel Eraslan, "Kadın birey olma savaşını kazanabilecek mi?" (Will woman win the battle of becoming an individual?), *Yeni Yüzyıl*, October 1, 1996.

26. Ali Bulaç, "Feminist bayanların aklı kısa" (Feminist women have small brains), *Zaman*, March 17, 1987; Mualla Gülnaz, "Ali Bulaç'ın düşündürdükleri" (What Ali Bulaç makes us think), *Zaman*, September 1, 1987; Mualla Gülnaz, "Biz kimiz?" (Who are we?), *Zaman*, September 15, 1987; Mualla Gülnaz, "Yolun sıfır kilometresinde" (At zero kilometers of the road), *Zaman*, October 20, 1987; Tuba Tuncer, "Kimin aklı kısa?" (Whose brain is small?), *Zaman*, September 15, 1987.

27. Sedef Öztürk, "Kadın Sorunu İslamcıların Gündeminde Nereye Kadar?" (How Far Does the Question of Woman Go in the Islamists' Agenda?), *Sosyalist Feminist Kaktüs*, 2, 1988, pp. 38–43.

28. Aysel Kurter et al., " 'Kadınlara Rağmen Kadınlar için' Tavrına Bir Eleştiri" (A Criticism of the 'For the Women Despite the Women' Attitude), *Sosyalist Feminist Kaktüs*, 4, 1988, pp. 25–27.

29. Sedef Öztürk, "Eleştiriye bir Yanıt" (A Response to Criticism), *Sosyalist Feminist Kaktüs*, 4, 1988, pp. 28–30.

30. Ruşen Çakır, *Direniş ve İtaat: İki İktidar Arasında İslamcı Kadın*, p. 58.

31. Yeşim Arat, "Feminism and Islam: Considerations on the Journal *Kadın ve Aile*," Şirin Tekeli (ed.), *Women in Modern Turkish Society*, London, Zed Press, 1991, pp. 66–78; Nilüfer Göle, *The Forbidden Modern: Civilization and Veiling*, Ann Arbor, The University of Michigan Press, 1996.

32. Elisabeth Özdalga, "Womanhood, Dignity and Faith: Reflections on an Islamic Woman's Life Story," *The European Journal of Women's Studies*, vol. 4, 1997, pp. 473–97; for other stories on the women who covered their heads, see Elisabeth Özdalga, *The Veiling Issue, Official Secularism and Popular Islam in Modern Turkey*, Surrey, Curzon Press, 1998.

33. On the unfolding of the headscarves saga, see Elizabeth Özdalga, *The Veiling Issue, Official Secularism and Popular Islam in Modern Turkey*, pp. 39–50; Ersin Kalaycıoğlu, "The Mystery of the 'Turban': Participation or Revolt?", paper presented at Tel Aviv University, December 8, 2003. For different comparative perspectives on the French headscarf dispute, see Anna Elisabetta Galeotti, "Citizenship and Equality: The Place for Toleration," *Political Theory*, 21:4, 1993, pp. 585–605; Norma Claire Moruzzi, "A Problem with Headscarves—Contemporary Complexities of Political and Social Identity," *Political Theory*, 22/4, 1994,

pp. 653–72; Levent Köker, "Political Toleration or Politics of Recognition: The Headscarves Affair Revisited," *Political Theory*, 24/2, 1996, pp. 315–20.

34. Cihan Aktaş, *Tesettür ve Toplum* (Islamic Covering and Society), İstanbul, Nehir Yayınları, 1992; Cihan Aktaş, *Tanzimattan Günümüze Kılık Kıyafet İktidar* (Attire and Power from the Tanzimat Reformation to Our Day), İstanbul, Nehir Yayınları, 1990; Nazife Şişman (ed.), *Başörtüsü Mağdurlarından Anlatılmamış Öyküler* (Untold Stories from the Victims of Headscarf), İstanbul, İz Yayınları, 1998; Nazife Şişman (ed.), *Kamusal Alanda Başörtülüler: Fatma Karabıyık Barbarasoğlu ile Söyleşi* (The Headscarved in Public Space: Interview with Fatma Karabıyık Barbarasoğlu), İstanbul, İz Yayıncılık, 2000; Elif Toros, "Hayat, Hikayeler ve Suskunluğa Dair" (Concerning Life, Stories and Silence) in Yıldız Ramazanoğlu (ed.), *Osmanlı'dan Cumhuriyet'e Kadının Tarihi Dönüşümü*, pp. 189–208.

35. The arguments summarized are abstracted from an official paper prepared by the Council of Higher Education and distributed within universities in 1998. The paper was named "Yükseköğretim kurumlarında kılık kıyafet ile ilgili mevzuat ve hukuki değerlendirmeler" (YKKM—Statutes and legal judgments concerning dress codes in institutions of higher education). All translations from this document are by Yeşim Arat. No author, no publisher.

36. YKKM, p. 3.

37. Ibid, p. 4.

38. Katherine Pratt Ewing, "Legislating Religious Freedom: Muslim Challenges to the Relationship between 'Church' and 'State' in Germany and France," *Daedalus*, 129, Fall 2000, p. 41.

39. YKKM, pp. 7–8.

40. In April 1999, the Fazilet Party that replaced the Refah Party could not have its headscarved deputy sworn in at the Turkish national assembly because of protests while in the assembly due to her wearing a headscarf. On this incident, see Fatma Müge Göçek, "To Veil or Not to Veil," *Interventions*, vol. 1, no. 4, pp. 521–35.

41. Yeşim Arat, "A Feminist Mirror in Turkey: Portraits of Two Activists in the 1980s," *Princeton Papers*, Fall 1996, vol. V, p. 122.

42. Ibid, p. 123.

43. Yeşim Arat, "The Project of Modernity and Women in Turkey," pp. 108–9.

44. Martha Minow, "About Women, About Culture: About Them, About Us," *Daedalus*, 129/4, Fall 2000, p. 131.

45. Yeşim Arat, "Feminists, Islamists and Political Change in Turkey," *Political Psychology*, 19/1, March 1998, p. 129.

46. Nesrin Tura, "*Pazartesi* Neye Karşı" (What is *Pazartesi* Against), *Pazartesi*, no. 25, April 1997, pp. 6–7.

## 2. REFAH PARTY AND THE ORGANIZATION OF THE LADIES' COMMISSIONS

1. Haldun Gülalp, "Political Islam in Turkey: The Rise and Fall of the Refah Party," *Muslim World*, January, LXXXIX/1, 1999, pp. 22–41; Haldun

Gülalp "Globalization and Political Islam," *International Journal of Middle East Studies*, 33/3, August 2001, pp. 433–48; Jeremy Salt, "Nationalism and the Rise of Muslim Sentiment in Turkey," *Middle Eastern Studies*, 31/1, 1993, pp. 13–27; Sencer Ayata, "The Rise of Islamic Fundamentalism and Its Institutional Framework" in A. Eralp, M. Tünay, and B. Yeşilada (eds.), *The Political and Socio-Economic Transformation of Turkey*, New York, Praeger, 1993, pp. 51–68; Sencer Ayata, "Patronage, Party and State—The Polarization of Islam in Turkey," *Middle East Journal*, 50/1, 1996, pp. 40–56.

2. Şerif Mardin, *Religion and Social Change in Modern Turkey*, Albany, State University of New York Press, 1989, p. 170.

3. İlkay Sunar and Binnaz Toprak, "Islam in Politics," *Government and Opposition*, 18, 1983, pp. 421–41.

4. Ümit Cizre-Sakallıoğlu, "Parameters and Strategies of Islam—State Interaction in Republican Turkey," *International Journal of Middle Eastern Studies*, 28, 1996, pp. 231–51.

5. Nilüfer Göle, *The Forbidden Modern: Civilization and Veiling*, Ann Arbor, University of Michigan Press, 1996; Nilüfer Göle, "Secularism and Islamism in Turkey: The Making of Elites and Counter-Elites," *Middle East Journal*, 51, 1997, p. 52.

6. Fuat Keyman, "On the Relation Between Global Modenity and Nationalism: The Crises of Hegemony and the Rise of (Islamic) Identity in Turkey," *New Perspectives on Turkey*, 13, 1995, pp. 93–120.

7. Binnaz Toprak, "Surviving Modernization: Islam as a Communal Means of Adaptation," *Il Politico*, 56, pp. 147–61.

8. Ziya Öniş, "The Political Economoy of Islamic Resurgence in Turkey: The Rise of the Welfare Party in Perspective," *Third World Quarterly*, 18/4, 1997, pp. 743–66.

9. *Refah Partisi Programı* (Program of the Welfare Party), Ankara, np. nd., pp. 6–7.

10. Binnaz Toprak, "Politicization of Islam in a Secular State: The National Salvation Party in Turkey" in Said Amir Arjomand (ed.), *From Nationalism to Revolutionary Islam*, Albany, New York, State University of New York Press, 1984, pp. 119–33; Ali Yaşar Sarıbay, *Türkiye'de Modernleşme Din ve Parti Politikası: "MSP Örnek Olayı,"* Istanbul, Alan Yayıncılık, 1985, pp. 89–101.

11. *Refah Partisi 24 Aralık 1995 Seçimleri Seçim Beyannamesi* (Welfare Party December 24, 1995 General Elections Election Declaration), np., nd., p. 4.

12. Ibid, pp. 4–5.

13. *Önce Ahlak ve Maneviyat* (First Morality and Morals), Refah Partisi, 1987, np. , p. 9.

14. Necmettin Erbakan, *Türkiye'nin Meseleleri ve Çözümleri* (Problems of Turkey and Their Solutions), Ankara, July 1991, p. 57.

15. Ibid, pp. 22–30.

16. Necmettin Erbakan, *Refah Partisi 4. Büyük Kongre Açış Konuşması* (Welfare Party 4th Congress Opening Speech), Ankara, Gümüş Matbaası, 10 October 1993, pp. 31–39.

17. Ibid, p. 42.

18. *Refah Partisi 24 Aralık 1995 Seçimleri Seçim Beyannamesi*, 1995, p. 29.

19. Necmettin Erbakan, *Türkiye'nin Meseleleri ve Çözümleri*, pp. 32–35.

20. *Milli Selamet Partisi Programı* (National Salvation Party Program), Ankara, nd., p. 9; Refah Partisi Programı (Welfare Party Program), Ankara, nd., p. 8.

21. *Refah Partisi 24 Aralık 1995 Seçimleri Seçim Beyannamesi*, 1995, pp. 30–31.

22. *Refah Partisi 20 Ekim 1991 Genel Seçimi Seçim Beyannamesi* (Welfare Party October 20 1991 General Elections Election Declaration), 1991, pp. 95–96.

23. *Refah Partisi 24 Aralık 1995 Seçimleri Seçim Beyannamesi*, 1995, pp. 20–22.

24. Haldun Gülalp, "Globalization and Political Islam: The Social Bases of Turkey's Welfare Party," *International Journal of Middle East Studies*, 33/3, 2001, pp. 433–48.

25. Binnaz Toprak, "Politicization of Islam in a Secular State: The National Salvation Party in Turkey," p. 132.

26. Ayşe Buğra, *Islam in Economic Organizations*, Istanbul, TESEV publication, 1999; Ayşe Öncü, "The Interaction of Politics, Religion and Finance: Islamic Banking in Turkey," paper presented at the Symposium on Muslims, Migrants and Metropolis, Berlin Institute for Comparative Social Research, Berlin, 1989.

27. Ayşe Buğra, "Class, Culture and State: An Analysis of Interest Representation by Two Turkish Business Associations," *International Journal of Middle East Studies*, 30/4, 1998.

28. Kemal Kirişçi and Gareth Winrow, *Kürt Sorunu: Kökeni ve Gelişimi* (Kurdish Question: Its Roots and Development), İstanbul, Tarih Vakfı Yurt Yayınları, 1997, p. 147.

29. Haldun Gülalp, "The Poverty of Democracy in Turkey: The Refah Party Episode," *New Perspectives on Turkey*, 21, Fall 1999, p. 41.

30. Ibid, p. 37.

31. Menderes Çınar argues that the Welfare Party ideology is similar to Kemalism in its authoritarian, statist outlook. See Menderes Çınar, "Postmodern Zamanların Kemalist Projesi," (Kemalist Project of the Postmodern Times), *Birikim*, November 1996, pp. 32–38.

32. To belittle the opposition in the parliament, Erbakan claimed that they were like the Africans, playing the drums and speaking gulu-gulu. *Sabah*, July 25, 1994.

33. Yeşim Arat, "Social Change and the 1983 Governing Elite in Turkey" in Mübeccel Kıray (ed.), *Structural Change in Turkish Society*, Indiana, Indiana University Turkish Studies, 1991, pp. 163–78.

34. Nilüfer Göle, "Secularism and Islamism in Turkey: The Making of Elites and Counter-Elites," *Middle East Journal*, 51/1, Winter 1997, pp. 46–58.

35. *Refah Partisi İstanbul İl Teşkilatı 1990 Yılı Çalışma Programı* (Welfare Party Istanbul Province 1990 Work Schedule), p. 6

36. Hakan Yavuz, "Political Islam and the Welfare (Refah) Party in Turkey," *Comparative Politics*, 30/1, October 1997, pp. 76–77.

37. *Refah Partisi Ankara İl Teşkilatı 1993 Yılı Çalışma Programı* (Welfare Party Ankara Province 1993 Work Schedule), pp. 18–21.

38. Ibid, pp. 34–39.

39. *Refah Partisi Istanbul İl Teşkilatı 1993 Yılı Çalışma Programı* (Welfare Party Istanbul Province 1993 Work Schedule), p. 34.

40. See *Teşkilat Rehberi RP* (Organization Guide Welfare Party), Ekim 1996 for further details.

41. *Refah Partisi Istanbul İl Teşkilatı 1993 Yılı Çalışma Programı*, p. 15.

42. *Teşkilat Rehberi, Refah Partisi,* 1996, p. 14; *Refah Partisi Ankara İl Teşkilatı 1993 Yılı Çalışma Programı*, p. 20.

43. These twenty-five units exhibited slight changes over time. This particular organizational schema was adapted from the information provided by the interviewees and the *Teşkilat Rehberi Refah Partisi,* October 1996.

44. *Teşkilat Rehberi, Refah Partisi,* 1996, p. 44; *Refah Partisi Ankara İl Teşkilatı 1993 Yılı Çalışma Programı*, p. 20.

45. *Refah Partisi Istanbul İl Teşkilatı 1993 Yılı Çalışma Programı*, p. 7.

46. *Refah Partisi Ankara İl Teşkilatı 1993 Yılı Çalışma Programı*, p. 7.

47. *Refah Partisi İstanbul İl Teşkilatı 1993 Yılı Çalışma Programı*, p. 12.

48. Ibid, pp. 13–14.

49. Ibid, p. 15.

50. Ibid, p. 24.

## 3. WOMEN IN THE ORGANIZATION

1. *Cumhuriyet*, January 6, 1987.

2. For a discussion of women who join the Islamist movement to pursue rights and authority that the traditional patriarchal society would not offer them, see Janet Afary, "Portraits of Two Islamist Women: Escape from Freedom or from Tradition?", *Critique,* 19, Fall 2001, pp. 47–77.

3. Thomas Franck, *The Empowered Self: Law and Society in the Age of Individualism,* New York, Oxford University Press, 1999, p. 1.

4. Ibid.

5. Catriona Mackenzie and Natalie Stoljar (eds.), *Relational Autonomy: Feminist Perspectives on Autonomy, Agency and the Social Self,* New York, Oxford University Press, 2000, p. 6.

6. Ibid.

7. On the different religious socialization experiences of women during the period of early Kemalist secularization process, see Aynur İlyasoğlu, "Religion and Women During the Course of Modernization in Turkey," *Oral History,* Autumn 1996, pp. 49–53.

8. On Islamist intellectuals, see Michael Meeker, "The New Muslim Intellectuals in the Republic of Turkey" in R. L. Tapper (ed.), *Islam in Modern Turkey: Religion, Politics and Literature in a Secular State,* London, I.B.Tauris, 1991, pp. 189–219; Binnaz Toprak, "Islamist Intellectuals: Revolt Against Industry and Technology" in Heper et al. (eds.), *Turkey and the West,* London, I.B.Tauris, 1993, pp. 237–57.

9. Joseph Raz, *The Morality of Freedom*, Oxford, Clarendon Press, 1986, pp. 369–70.

10. Belgin Tekçe introduces the concept of "embedded conjugality" to describe marriages where connections to other kin are significant. See Belgin Tekçe, *On Routes to Marriage*, HCPD Working Paper Series, vol. 12, 7, 2002.

11. Bernard Lewis, *The Emergence of Modern Turkey*, London, Oxford University Press, 1976 (third printing), p. 268.

12. The number of female students in junior high school level religious education increased from 19,277 in the 1984–85 school year to 71,630 in 1991–92. At the senior high school level, the number of female students in religious education increased from 12,338 in the 1984–85 school year to 31, 917 in 1991–92, *Statistical Yearbook of Turkey 1993*, State Institute of Statistics Prime Ministry Republic of Turkey, 1993, pp. 164–66.

13. *Milli Gazete*, July 7, 1995, December 15, 1995.

14. Valerie J. Hoffman, "An Islamic Activist: Zaynab-al-Ghazali" in Elizabeth W. Fernea (ed.), *Women and the Family in the Middle East*, Austin, University of Texas Press, 1985, pp. 233–54.

15. *Hürriyet*, March 30, 1994.

16. *Pazartesi*, September 1995, p. 2–5; Cathy Benton, "Many Contradictions: Women and Islamists in Turkey," *Muslim World*, vol. 86, no. 2, 1996, pp. 106–27.

## 4. MOBILIZING FOR THE PARTY

1. *İstanbul 6. Olağan İl Kongresi Faaliyet Raporu* (6th Istanbul Province Ordinary Congress Activity Report), p. 12. The mahalle is the smallest administrative unit and includes a number of streets. The counties and districts are progressively larger units.

2. "İstanbul İl Hanımlar Komisyonu Çalışma Raporu" (Istanbul Province Ladies' Commission Work Report), unpublished report prepared by Handan Bayer, September 3, 1997.

3. *İstanbul 6. Olağan İl Kongresi Faaliyet Raporu*, p. 35.

4. Ibid, p. 13.

5. We have been told that the highest number of women members were registered in Istanbul. Ankara followed with about 250,000 women members by the time the party closed.

6. Unpublished report, courtesy of Sadık Albayrak, Istanbul, 1992, p. 2.

7. A gold inscription written in Arabic that asks for God's protection and is usually given to newborn babies to avert the evil eye.

8. *İstanbul 6. Olağan İl Kongresi Faaliyet Raporu*, p. 35.

9. *Milli Gazete*, October 22, 1995.

10. *Milli Gazete*, October 26, 1993.

11. *Milli Gazete*, October 23, 1994.

12. *Milli Gazete*, November 24, 1994.

13. *Milli Gazete*, December 23, 1993.

14. *Milli Gazete*, July 23, 1995.

15. *Milli Gazete,* January 16, 1994.

16. *Milli Gazete,* August 4, 1995.

17. *Milli Gazete,* August 8, 1994; *Milli Gazete,* August 24, 1994.

18. *Milli Gazete,* August 8, 1994.

19. *Milli Gazete,* December 23, 1993.

20. *Cumhuriyet,* February 17, 1994.

21. *Büyük Larousse Sözlük ve Ansiklopedisi,* vol. 17, İstanbul, Milliyet Yayınları, 1986, p. 8594.

22. *Milli Gazete,* August 24, 1994.

23. *Milli Gazete,* January 20, 1996.

24. *Milli Gazete,* December 23, 1995.

25. *Milli Gazete,* December 20, 1993.

26. *Milli Gazete,* December 23, 1993.

27. *Milli Gazete,* December 21, 1994.

28. *Milli Gazete,* December 21, 1994.

29. *Milli Gazete,* October 26, 1993.

30 *Milli Gazete,* August 21, 1994.

31. *Milli Gazete,* March 20, 1995.

32. Interpersonal relations were significant for the party in general, not merely for the women's commissions. See Jenny B. White, "Islam and Democracy: The Turkish Experience," *Current History,* January 1995, p. 11.

33. For a similar practice among lower-class women in Egypt, see Diane Singerman, *Avenues of Participation: Family, Politics and Networks in Urban Quarters of Cairo,* Princeton, N.J., Princeton University Press, 1995.

34. Hakan Yavuz, "Political Islam and the Welfare (Refah) Party in Turkey," *Comparative Politics,* 30/ 1, October 1997, p. 78–80.

35. Ildiko Beller-Hann, "Prostitution and Its Effects in Northeast Turkey," *The European Journal of Women's Studies,* 2, 1995, p. 219–35.

36. *Milli Gazete,* December 13, 1993.

37. Ibid.

38. Ildiko Beller-Hann, "Prostitution and Its Effects in Northeast Turkey," pp. 225–26.

39. The daily newspaper *Sabah* reported on the Refah Party's success in the region with the caption "Nataşa's favoritism to Refah." (Nataşa is used as a generic name for Russian prostitutes.) See *Sabah,* March 29, 1994.

## 5. WORLDVIEWS OF REFAH WOMEN

1. Nükte Devrim Bouvard, "Turkish Women and the Welfare Party," *Middle East Report,* April–June 1996, p. 29; *Cumhuriyet,* January 6, 1987.

2. Ayşe Saktanber, "Becoming the 'Other' as a Muslim in Turkey: Turkish Women vs. Islamist Women," *New Perspectives on Turkey,* 11, 1994, pp. 99–134.

3. Ann Elizabeth Mayer, "Universal Versus Islamic Human Rights: A Clash of Cultures or a Clash with a Construct?", *Michigan Journal of International Law,* 15, 1994, pp 307–404; Ann Elizabeth Mayer, "Cultural Particularism

as a Bar to Women's Rights. Reflections on the Middle Eastern Experience" in Julie Peters and Andrea Wolper (eds.), *Women's Rights, Human Rights: International Feminist Perspectives*, Routledge, 1995, pp. 176–88.

4. *Yeni Yüzyıl*, November 30, 1995.

5. On the problems of integrating Islamists and minority groups within liberal democracies, see Susan Okin et al., *Is Multiculturalism Bad for Women?*, Princeton, N.J., Princeton University Press, 1999.

6. Bahattin Akşit, "Islamic Education in Turkey: Medrese Reform in Late Ottoman Times and Imam-Hatip Schools in the Republic" in Richard Tapper (ed.), *Islam in Modern Turkey*, London, I.B.Tauris, 1991, pp. 145–70. The junior high schools were closed in 1998 when eight-year elementary education became obligatory for young children.

7. Buket Türkmen, "Laikliğin Dönüşümü: Liseli Gençler, Türban ve Atatürk Rozeti" (The Transformation of Secularism: High School Youth, Headscarf and the Atatürk Badge) in Nilüfer Göle (ed.), *İslamın Yeni Kamusal Yüzleri*, (The New Public Faces of Islam), İstanbul, Metis Yayınları, 2000, pp. 110–47.

8. Feride Acar and Ayşe Ayata, "Discipline, Success and Stability: The Reproduction of Gender and Class in Turkish Secondary Education" in Deniz Kandiyoti and Ayşe Saktanber (eds.), *Fragments of Culture*, London, I.B.Tauris, 2002, pp. 90–111.

9. On the changing Islamic discourses on women and gender, see Leila Ahmed, *Women and Gender in Islam*, New Haven, Conn., Yale University Press, 1992, pp. 64–78; on a critical study of selected Islamic human rights documents including those related to women, see Ann Elizabeth Mayer, *Islam and Human Rights*, Boulder, Colo. Westview Press, 1991; on a contextual interpretation of the inferior status of women in the Quran, see Fazlur Rahman, "Status of Women in the Quran" in Guity Nashat (ed.),*Women and Revolution in Iran*, Boulder, Colo., Westview Press, 1983, pp. 37–54; on a feminist defense of Islam and multiculturalism against its critics, see Azizah Al Hibri, "Is Western Patriarchal Feminism Good for Third World/Minority Women?" in Susan Okin et al., *Is Multiculturalism Bad For Women*, Princeton, N.J., Princeton University Press, 1999, pp. 41–46.

10. Fazlur Rahman, "Status of Women in the Quran" in Guity Nashat (ed.), *Women and Revolution in Iran*, Boulder, Colo., Westview Press, 1983, pp. 37–54. According to Rahman, Muslims cannot practice polygamy in present-day circumstances. Polygamy came to be practiced in a context where the wars of the early years of Islam left many widows needy of male protection; furthermore, there was an explicit warning in the Quran that unless you can do justice to each wife, which was humanly impossible, you marry only one.

11. See, for example, Hüseyin Hatemi, *Kadının Çıkış Yolu* (Women's Way to Salvation), Ankara, Fecr Yayınevi, 1988, pp. 43–59.

12. Secular intellectuals have made the parallel but opposite argument that Islamists and Kemalists share the same patriarchal view toward women and see the latter as second-class citizens. See Ahmet İnsel, "Refah Partisi ve Kemalism" (Welfare Party and Kemalism), *Birikim*, vol. 81, 1996, pp. 29–31.

13. Azizah Al Hibri (ed.), *Women and Islam*, Oxford, Pergamon Press, 1982; Barbara Fryer Stowasser, "Liberated Equal or Protected Dependent? Contemporary Religious Paradigms on Women's Status in Islam," *Arab Studies Quarterly*, Summer 1987, pp. 260–83.

14. On the alternative consumption culture of Islamists, see Yael Navaro-Yashin, "The Market for Identities: Secularism, Islamism, Commodities" in Deniz Kandiyoti and Ayşe Saktanber (eds.), *Fragments of Culture*, London, I.B.Tauris, 2002, pp. 221–53.

15. Public opinion survey conducted by Ali Çarkoğlu and Binnaz Toprak had similar findings in which respondents who claimed that they wanted Islamic law also opposed specific dictates of Islamic law. According to this survey, 21.2 percent of the respondents wanted a religious state based on Islamic law. However, only 1.4 percent believed that in cases of adultery the guilty should be punished according to Quranic dictates. See Ali Çarkoğlu and Binnaz Toprak, *Türkiye'de Din Toplum ve Siyaset*, (Religion, Society and Politics in Turkey) Istanbul, TESEV Yayınları, 2000.

## CONCLUSION

1. Clifford Geertz, *Available Light*, Princeton, N.J., Princeton University Press, 2000, p. 258.

2. Mark Warren, *Democracy and Association*, Princeton, N.J., Princeton University Press, 2001, pp. 70–75.

3. Quoted in Micheline R. Malson et al. (eds.), *Feminist Theory in Practice and Process*, Chicago, University of Chicago Press, 1989, p. 8.

4. Martha C. Nussbaum, *Women and Human Development: The Capabilities Approach*, Cambridge, MA, Cambridge University Press, 2000, p. 182.

5. Clifford Geertz, *Available Light*, p. 258.

6. Martha C. Nussbaum, "A Plea for Difficulty" in S. Okin et al. (eds.), *Is Multiculturalism Bad for Women*, Princeton, NJ, Princeton University Press, 1999, p. 106; Will Kymlicka, *Multicultural Citizenship: A Liberal Theory of Minority Rights*, Oxford, Clarendon Press, 1995.

7. Refah women could not be compared to the feminists within the church that Mary Fainsod Katzenstein writes about in *Faithful and Fearless: Moving Feminist Protest Inside the Church and Military*, Princeton, N.J., Princeton University Press, 1998.

8. Bhikhu Parekh, *Rethinking Multiculturalism*, Cambridge, Mass., Harvard University Press, 2002, (2d ed.) p. 113.

# Bibliography

## BOOKS, ARTICLES AND THESES

Abadan-Unat, Nermin. (1981) "Social Change and Turkish Women," in N. Abadan Unat (ed.), *Women in Turkish Society*, Leiden, E. J. Brill, 5–31.

Acar, Feride. (1983) "Turkish Women in Academia: Roles and Careers," *METU Studies in Development*, 10, 409–46.

———. (1991) "Women in the Ideology of Islamic Revivalism in Turkey: Three Islamic Women's Journals," in R. L.Tapper (ed.), *Islam in Modern Turkey: Religion Politics and Literature in a Secular State*, London, I.B.Tauris, 280–303.

Acar, Feride and Ayşe Ayata. (2002) "Discipline, Success and Stability: The Reproduction of Gender and Class in Turkish Secondary Education" in Deniz Kandiyoti and Ayşe Saktanber (eds.), *Fragments of Culture*, London, I.B.Tauris, 90–111.

Afary, Janet. (2001) "Portraits of Two Islamist Women: Escape from Freedom or from Tradition," *Critique*, 19, Fall, 47–77.

Ahmad, Feroz. (1991) "The Progressive Republican Party, 1923–1945," in Metin Heper and Jacob Landau (eds.), *Political Parties and Democracy in Turkey*, London, I.B.Tauris, 65–82.

Ahmad, Feroz. (1993) *The Making of Modern Turkey*, London, Routledge.

Akşit, Bahattin. (1991) "Islamic Education in Turkey: Medrese Reform in Late Ottoman Times and Imam-Hatip Schools in the Republic," in R. L. Tapper (ed.), *Islam in Modern Turkey: Religion, Politics and Literature in a Secular State*, London, I.B.Tauris, 145–69.

Aktaş, Cihan. (1986) *Kadının Serüveni* (Adventure of Woman), İstanbul, Girişim Yayıncılık.

———. (1990) *Tanzimattan Günümüze Kılık Kıyafet İktidar* (Attire and Power from the Tanzimat Reformation to Our Day), İstanbul, Nehir.

———. (1992) *Tesettür ve Toplum* (Islamic Covering and Society), İstanbul, Nehir.

Al Hibri, Azizah Y. (1999) "Is Western Patriarchal Feminism Good for Third World/ Minority Women?" in Susan Okin et al., *Is Multiculturalism Bad for Women?*, Princeton, N.J., Princeton University Press, 41–46.

Arat,Yeşim. (1989) *Patriarchal Paradox: Women Politicians in Turkey*, Madison, N.J., Fairleigh Dickinson University Press.

———. (1991) "Feminism and Islam: Considerations on the Journal *Kadın ve Aile*" in Şirin Tekeli (ed.), *Women in Modern Turkish Society*, London, Zed Press, 66–78.

———. (1991) "Social Change and the 1983 Governing Elite in Turkey" in Mübeccel Kıray (ed.), *Structural Change in Turkish Society*, Indiana, Indiana University Turkish Studies, 163–78.

———. (1996) "A Feminist Mirror in Turkey: Portraits of Two Activists in the 1980s," *Princeton Papers*, 5, Fall, 113–32.

———. (1997) "The Project of Modernity and Women in Turkey" in Sibel Bozdoğan and Reşat Kasaba (eds.), *Rethinking Modernity and National Identity in Turkey*, Seattle, University of Washington Press, 95–112.

———. (1998) "Feminists, Islamists and Political Change in Turkey," *Political Psychology*, 19/1, 117–32.

———. (1999) *Political Islam in Turkey and Women's Organizations*. Istanbul, TESEV.

Arat, Zehra. (1994) "Turkish Women and the Republican Reconstruction of Tradition" in Fatma Müge Göçek and Shiva Balaghi (eds.), *Reconstructing Gender in the Middle East*, New York, Columbia University Press, 57–78.

Ayata, Sencer. (1993) "The Rise of Islamic Fundamentalism and Its Institutional Framework" in A. Eralp, M. Tünay, and B. Yeşilada (eds.), *The Political and Socio-Economic Transformation of Turkey*, New York, Praeger, 51–68.

———. (1996) "Patronage, Party and State-The Polarization of Islam in Turkey," *Middle East Journal*, 50/1, 40–56.

Beller-Hann, Ildiko. (1995) "Prostitution and Its Effects in Northeast Turkey," *The European Journal of Women's Studies*, 2, 219–35.

Benhabib, Seyla. (2002) "Unholy Politics," in *Constellations: An International Journal of Critical and Democratic Theory*, March, 34–45.

———. (2002) *The Claims of Culture*, Princeton and Oxford, Princeton University Press.

Benton, Cathy. (1996) "Many Contradictions: Women and Islamists in Turkey," *Muslim World*, 86/2, 106–127.

Berkes, Niyazi. (1964) *The Development of Secularism in Turkey*, Montreal, McGill University Press.

Birtek, Faruk and Binnaz Toprak. (1993) "The Conflictual Agendas of Neo-Liberal Reconstruction and the Rise of Islamic Politics in Turkey: The Hazards of Rewriting Modernity," *Praxis International*, July, 192–212.

Buğra, Ayşe. (1998) "Class, Culture and State: An Analysis of Two Turkish Business Associations," *International Journal of Middle Eastern Studies*, 30/4, 521–39.

———. (1999) *Islam in Economic Organizations*, Istanbul, TESEV.

Bulaç, Ali. (1987) "Feminist bayanların aklı kısa," (Feminist women have small brains) *Zaman*, March 17.

*Büyük Larousse Sözlük ve Ansiklopedisi*. (1986) Istanbul, Milliyet Yayınları.

Carroll, S. and Linda Zerilli. (1993) "Feminist Challenges to Political Science," in Ada Finifer (ed.), *Political Science: The State of the Discipline II*, Washington, D.C., The American Political Science Association, 55–76.

Çakır, Ruşen. (1994) *Ne Şeriat Ne Demokrasi* (Neither Shariat Nor Democracy), İstanbul, Metis Yayınları.

———. (2000) *Direniş ve İtaat: İki İktidar Arasında İslamcı Kadın* (Resistance and Obedience: Islamist Woman Between Two Authorities), İstanbul, Metis Yayınları.

Çakır, Serpil. (1993) *Osmanlı Kadın Hareketi* (Ottoman Women's Movement), İstanbul, Metis Yayınları.

Çarkoğlu, Ali and Binnaz Toprak. (2000) *Türkiye'de Din, Toplum ve Siyaset* (Religion, Society and Politics in Turkey), İstanbul, TESEV Yayınları.

Çiftçi, Halise. (1996) "Bizim feministlerden değil, onların bizden alacakları çok şey var" (There is a lot feminists can take from us, not us from them), *Milli Gazete*, February 16.

Çınar, Alev İnan. (1997) "Refah Party and the City Administration of Istanbul: Liberal Islam, Localism and Hybridity," *New Perspectives on Turkey*, 16, Spring, 23–40.

Çınar, Menderes. (1996) "Postmodern Zamanların Kemalist Projesi" (Kemalist Project of the Postmodern Times) *Birikim*, November, 32–38.

Cizre-Sakallıoğlu, Ümit. (1996) "Parameters and Strategies of Islam-State Interaction in Republican Turkey," *International Journal of Middle Eastern Studies*, 28, 231–51.

*Cumhuriyet*. (1987) January 6.

*Cumhuriyet*. (1994) February 17.

Davison, Andrew. (1998) *Secularism and Revivalism in Turkey*, New Haven, Conn., Yale University Press.

Devrim-Bouvard, Nükte. (1996) "Turkish Women and the Welfare Party," *Middle East Report*, April–June, 28–29.

Durakbaşa, Ayşe. (1988) "Cumhuriyet Döneminde Kemalist Kadın Kimliğinin Oluşumu" (The Formation of Kemalist Woman's Identity in the Republican Period), *Tarih ve Toplum*, 51, 39–43.

Eraslan, Sibel. (1996) "Kadın birey olma savaşını kazanabilecek mi?" (Will woman win the battle of becoming an individual?) *Yeni Yüzyıl*, October 1.

Esmer, Yılmaz. (2003) "Is There an Islamic Civilization" in Ronald Inglehart (ed.), *Human Values and Social Change*, Leiden, E. J. Brill, 35–68.

Ewing, Katherine Pratt. (2000) "Legislating Religious Freedom: Muslim Challenges to the Relationship Between 'Church' and 'State' in Germany and France," *Daedalus*, 129, Fall, 31–54.

Franck, Thomas. (1999) *The Empowered Self: Law and Society in the Age of Individualism*, New York, Oxford University Press.

Galeotti, Anna Elisabetta. (1993) "Citizenship and Equality: The Place for Toleration," *Political Theory*, 21/4, 585–605.

Geertz, Clifford. (1973) *Interpretation of Cultures*, New York, Basic Books.

———. (2000) *Available Light*, Princeton, N.J., Princeton University Press.

Göçek, Müge. (1999) "To Veil or Not to Veil," *Interventions*, 1/4, 521–35.

Gökalp, Ziya. (1968) *Türkçülüğün Esasları* (Principles of Turkism), İstanbul, Varlık Yayınları.

Göle, Nilüfer. (1996) *The Forbidden Modern: Civilization and Veiling*, Ann Arbor, University of Michigan Press.

———. (1996) "Authoritarian Secularism and Islamist Politics: The Case of Turkey," *Civil Society in the Middle East*, Leiden, E. J. Brill, 17–43.

———. (1997) "Secularism and Islamism in Turkey: The Making of Elites and Counter-Elites," *Middle East Journal*, 51/1, 46–58.

——— (ed.) (2000) *İslamın Yeni Kamusal Yüzleri* (The New Public Faces of Islam), İstanbul, Metis Yayınları.

Gülalp, Haldun. (1992) "A Postmodern Reaction to Dependent Moderniza-tion: The Social and Historical Roots of Islamic Radicalism," *New Per-spectives on Turkey*, 8, Fall, 15–26.

———. (1999) "Political Islam in Turkey: The Rise and Fall of the Refah Party," *Muslim World*, 89/1, 22–41.

———. (1999) "The Poverty of Democracy in Turkey: The Refah Party Epi-sode," *New Perspectives on Turkey*, 21, Fall, 35–60 .

———. (2001) "Globalization and Political Islam," *International Journal of Middle East Studies*, 33/3, 433–48.

Gülnaz, Mualla. (1987) "Ali Bulaç'ın düşündürdükleri" (What Ali Bulaç makes us think), *Zaman*, September 1.

———. (1987) "Biz kimiz?" (Who are we?), *Zaman*, September 15.

———. (1987) "Yolun sıfır kilometresinde," (At zero kilometers of the road), *Zaman*, October 20.

Hatemi, Hüseyin. (1988) *Kadının Çıkış Yolu* (Women's Way to Salvation), Ankara, Fecr Yayınevi.

Heper, Metin. (1985) *The State Tradition in Turkey*, Walkington, Eothen.

———. (1997) "Islam and Democracy in Turkey: Toward a Reconciliation," *Middle East Journal*, 51/1, 32–45.

Hoffman, Valerie. (1985) "An Islamic Activist: Zaynab-al-Ghazali" in Eliza-beth Fernea (ed.), *Women and the Family in the Middle East*, Austin, University of Texas Press, 233–54.

Huntington, Samuel. (1996) *The Clash of Civilizations and the Remaking of World Order*, New York, Simon and Schuster.

*Hürriyet*. (1994) "Tayyip'i başkanlığa taşıyan RP'li kadın" (Welfare Party woman who led Tayyip to mayoralty), March 30.

İlyasoğlu, Aynur. (1994) *Örtülü Kimlik* (Veiled Identity), İstanbul, Metis Yayınları.

———. (1996) "Religion and Women During the Course of Modernization in Turkey," *Oral History*, Autumn, 49–53.

İnan, Afet. (1959) *Atatürk Hakkında Hatıralar ve Belgeler* (Documents and Memo-ries on Atatürk), Ankara, Türk Tarih Kurumu Basımevi.

İnsel, Ahmet. (1996) "Refah Partisi ve Kemalism" (Welfare Party and Kemalism), *Birikim*, 91, 29–31.

Kalaycıoğlu, Ersin. (2003) "The Mystery of the 'Turban': Participation or Re-volt?", paper presented at Tel Aviv University, December 8.

Kandiyoti, Deniz. (1988) "Bargaining with Patriarchy," *Gender and Society*, 2/3, 274–90.

———. (1989) "Women and the Turkish State: Political Actors or Symbolic Pawns?" in Nira Yuval-Davis and Floya Anthias (eds.), *Women–Nation–State*, London, The Macmillan Press, 126–49.

————. (1991) "End of Empire: Islam, Nationalism and Women in Turkey," in D. Kandiyoti (ed.), *Women, Islam and the State*, Philadelphia, Temple University Press, 22–47.

————. (1991) "Identity and Its Discontents: Women and the Nation," *Millennium: Journal of International Studies*, 20/3, 429–43.

Katzenstein, Mary Fainsod. (1998) *Faithful and Fearless: Moving Feminist Protest inside the Church and Military*, Princeton, N.J., Princeton University Press.

Keyder, Çağlar. (1987) *State and Class in Turkey*, London, Verso.

Keyman, Fuat. (1995) "On The Relation Between Global Modernity and Nationalism: The Crises of Hegemony and The Rise of (Islamic) Identity in Turkey," *New Perspectives on Turkey*, 13, 93–120.

Kirişçi, Kemal and Gareth Winrow. (1997) *Kürt Sorunu: Kökeni ve Gelişimi* (Kurdish Question: Its Roots and Development), İstanbul, Tarih Vakfı Yayınları.

Köker, Levent. (1996) "Political Toleration or Politics of Recognition: The Headscarves Affair Revisited," *Political Theory*, 24/2, 315–20.

Kurter, Aysel et al., (1988) " 'Kadınlara Rağmen Kadınlar İçin' Tavrına Bir Eleştiri" (A Criticism of the 'For the Women Despite the Women' Attitude), *Sosyalist Feminist Kaktüs*, 4, 25–27.

Kymlicka, Will. (1995) *Multicultural Citizenship: A Liberal Theory of Minority Rights*, Oxford, Clarendon Press.

————. (2001) *Politics in the Vernacular: Nationalism, Multiculturalism and Citizenship*, Oxford, New York, Oxford University Press.

Kymlicka, Will and Wayne Norman (eds.) (2000) *Citizenship in Diverse Societies*, Oxford, New York, Oxford University Press.

Lewis, Bernard. (1976) *The Emergence of Modern Turkey*, London, Oxford University Press.

Mackenzie, Catriona and Natalie Stoljar (eds.). (2000) *Relational Autonomy: Feminist Perspectives on Autonomy, Agency and the Social Self*, New York, Oxford University Press.

Malson, Micheline et al. (eds.). (1989) *Feminist Theory in Practice and Process*, Chicago, The University of Chicago Press.

Mardin, Şerif. (1981) "Religion and Secularism in Turkey," in Ali Kazancıgil and E. Özbudun (eds.), *Atatürk: Founder of a Modern State*, London, C. Hirst. 191–219.

————. (1983) *Jön Türklerin Siyasi Fikirleri* (The Political Ideas of the Young Turks), İstanbul, İletişim Yayınları.

————. (1989) *Religion and Social Change in Modern Turkey*, Albany, State University of New York.

————. (1994) "Islam in Mass Society: Harmony versus Polarization," in Heper and Evin (eds.), *Politics in the Third Turkish Republic*, Boulder, Colo., Westview Press, 161–68.

Mayer, Ann Elizabeth. (1991) *Islam and Human Rights*, Boulder, Colo., Westview Press.

————. (1994) "Universal Versus Islamic Human Rights: A Clash of Cultures or a Clash with a Construct?", *Michigan Journal of International Law*, 15, 307–404.

————. (1995) "Cultural Particularism as a Bar to Women's Rights. Reflections on the Middle Eastern Experience," in Julie Peters and Andrea Wolper (eds.), *Women's Rights, Human Rights: International Feminist Perspectives,* Routledge, 176–88.

Meeker, Michael E. (1991) "The New Muslim Intellectuals in the Republic of Turkey," in R. L. Tapper (ed.), *Islam in Modern Turkey: Religion, Politics and Literature in a Secular State,* London, I.B.Tauris, 189–219.

*Milli Gazete.* (1993) October 26; December 13; December 20; December 23, December 29.

*Milli Gazete.* (1994) January 16; February 16; August 8; August 21; August 24; October 23; November 24; December 21.

*Milli Gazete.* (1995) March 20; July 7; July 23; August 4; October 22; December 15; December 23.

Minow, Martha. (2000) "About Women, About Culture: About Them, About Us," *Daedalus,* 129/4, Fall, 125–45.

Moruzzi, Norma Claire. (1994) "A Problem with Headscarves—Contemporary Complexities of Political and Social Identity," *Political Theory,* 22/4, 653–72.

Navaro, Yael. (1991) " 'Using the Mind' at Home: The Rationalization of Housewifery in Early Republican Turkey (1928–1940)," honors thesis submitted to the Department of Sociology, Brandeis University.

Navaro-Yashin, Yael. (2002) "The Market for Identities: Secularism, Islamism, Commodities," in Deniz Kandiyoti and Ayşe Saktanber (eds.), *Fragments of Culture,* London, I.B.Tauris, 221–53.

————. (2002) *Faces of the State: Secularism and Public Life in Turkey,* Princeton, N.J., Princeton University Press.

Nussbaum, Martha C. (1999) "A Plea for Difficulty" in Susan Okin et al. (eds.), *Is Multiculturalism Bad for Women,* Princeton, N.J., Princeton University Press, 105–114.

————. (2001) *Women and Human Development,* Cambridge, Mass., Cambridge University Press.

Okin, Susan et al. (1999) *Is Multiculturalism Bad for Women,* Princeton, N.J., Princeton University Press.

Öncü, Ayşe. (1981) "Turkish Women in the Professions: Why So Many?" in Nermin Abadan Unat (ed.), *Women in Turkish Society,* Leiden, E. J. Brill, 180–93.

————. (1989) "The Interaction of Politics, Religion and Finance: Islamic Banking in Turkey," paper presented at the Symposium on Muslims, Migrants and Metropolis, Berlin Institute for Compariative Social Research, Berlin.

Öniş, Ziya. (1997) "The Political Economy of Islamic Resurgence In Turkey: The Rise of The Welfare Party in Perspective," *Third World Quarterly,* 18/4, 743–66.

————. (2001) "Political Islam at the crossroads: from hegemony to co-existence," *Contemporary Politics,* 7/4, 281–98.

Özdalga, Elisabeth. (1997) "Womanhood, Dignity and Faith: Reflections on an Islamic Woman's Life Story," *The European Journal of Women's Studies*, 4, 473–97.

———. (1998) *The Veiling Issue, Official Secularism and Popular Islam in Modern Turkey*, Surrey, Curzon Press.

Öztürk, Sedef. (1988) "Kadın Sorunu İslamcıların Gündeminde Nereye Kadar?" (How Far Does the Question of Woman Go in the Islamists' Agenda?), *Sosyalist Feminist Kaktüs*, 2, 38–43.

———. (1988) "Eleştiriye bir Yanıt," (A Response to Criticism), *Sosyalist Feminist Kaktüs*, 4, 28–30.

Özyürek, Esra. (2000) "Mecliste Başörtüsü Düğümü" (The Headscarf Knot in the Parliament), in Ayşegül Altınay (ed.), *Vatan, Millet, Kadınlar* (Country, Nation, Women), İstanbul, İletişim Yayınları, 339–57.

Parekh, Bhikhu. (2002) *Rethinking Multiculturalism: Cultural Diversity and Political Theory*, Cambridge, Mass., Harvard University Press.

*Pazartesi.* (1995) September.

Pusch, Barbara. (2000) "Stepping into the Public Sphere: The Rise of Islamist and Religious Conservative Women's Non-Governmental Organizations," in Stefanos Yerasimos et al. (eds.), *Civil Society in the Grip of Nationalism*, Istanbul, Orient Institute.

Rahman, Fazlur. (1983) "Status of Women in the Quran" in G. Nashat (ed.), *Women and Revolution in Iran*, Boulder, Colo., Westview Press, 37–54.

Ramazanoğlu, Yıldız. (2000) "Yol Ayrımında İslamcı ve Feminist Kadınlar" (Islamist and Feminist Women at the Crossroads), in Yıldız Ramazanoğlu (ed.), *Osmanlı'dan Cumhuriyet'e Kadının Tarihi Dönüşümü* (The Historical Transformation of Woman from Ottoman Times to the Republic), İstanbul, Pınar Yayınları, 139–67.

Raz, Joseph. (1986) *The Morality of Freedom*, Oxford, Clarendon Press.

*Sabah.* (1994) July 25; March 29.

Saktanber, Ayşe. (1994) "Becoming the 'Other' as a Muslim in Turkey: Turkish Women vs. Islamist Women," *New Perspectives on Turkey*, 11, 99–134.

———. (2002) *Living Islam: Women, Religion and the Politicization of Culture in Turkey*, London, I.B.Tauris.

Salt, Jeremy. (1995) "Nationalism and the Rise of Muslim Sentiment in Turkey," *Middle Eastern Studies*, 31/1, 13–27.

———. (1999) "Turkey's Military 'Democracy,' " *Current History*, February, 72–78.

Sarıbay, Ali Yaşar. (1985) *Türkiye'de Modernleşme, Din ve Parti Politikası: "MSP Örnek Olayı"* (Modernization, Religion and Party Politics in Turkey: The MSP Case), İstanbul, Alan Yayıncılık.

Sevindi, Nevval. (1996) "Refah'ın Kadınları" (Welfare Party Women), *Yeni Yüzyıl*, August 26–30.

———. (1996) "Kadınlar RP'de 2. sınıf" (Women are second class in th Welfare Party), *Yeni Yüzyıl*, October 12.

———. (1996) "Refahlı kadınlar güçlerinin farkında değil" (Welfare Party women are not aware of their power), *Yeni Yüzyıl*, October 15.

Singerman, Diane. (1995) *Avenues of Participation: Family, Politics and Networks in Urban Quarters of Cairo*, Princeton, N.J., Princeton University Press.

Sirman, Nükhet. (1989) "Feminism in Turkey: A Short History," *New Perspectives on Turkey*, 3, 1–34.

Şişman, Nazife (ed.) (1998) *Başörtüsü Mağdurlarından Anlatılmamış Öyküler* (Untold Stories from Headscarf Victims), İstanbul, İz Yayıncılık.

——— (ed.) (2000) *Kamusal Alanda Başörtülüler: Fatma Karabıyık Barbarosoğlu ile Söyleşi* (The Headscarved in Public Space: Interview with Fatma Karabıyık Barbarosoğlu), İstanbul, İz Yayıncılık.

*Statistical Yearbook of Turkey*. (1993) State Institute of Statistics Prime Ministry Republic of Turkey.

Stowasser, Barbara Fryer. (1987) "Liberated Equal or Protected Dependent? Contemporary Religious Paradigms on Women's Status in Islam," *Arab Studies Quarterly*, Summer, 260–83.

Sunar, İlkay and Binnaz Toprak. (1983) "Islam in Politics," *Government and Opposition*, 18, 421–41.

Tapper, R. L. (ed.) (1991) *Islam in Modern Turkey: Religion, Politics and Literature in a Secular State*, London, I.B.Tauris.

Taylor, Charles, et al. (1994) *Multiculturalism*, Princeton, N.J., Princeton University Press.

Tekçe, Belgin. (2002) *On Routes to Marriage*, Harvard Center for Population and Development Working Paper Series, vol. 12, 7.

Tekeli, Şirin. (1986) "Emergence of the Feminist Movement in Turkey," in Drude Dahlerup (ed.), *The New Women's Movement: Feminism and Political Power in Europe and the USA*, London, Sage Publications, 179–99.

———. (1990) "Women in the Changing Political Associations of the 1980s," in Andrew Finkel and Nükhet Sirman (eds.), *Turkish State, Turkish Society*, London, Routledge, 259–88.

Toprak, Binnaz. (1981) *Islam and Political Development in Turkey*, Leiden, E. J. Brill.

———. (1984) "Politicization of Islam in a Secular State: The National Salvation Party in Turkey" in Said Amir Arjomand (ed.), *From Nationalism to Revolutionary Islam*, Albany, State University of New York Press, 119–33.

———. (1991) "Surviving Modernization: Islam as a Communal Means of Adaptation," *Il Politico*, 56, 147–61.

———. (1993) "Islamist Intellectuals: Revolt against Industry and Technology," in Heper et al. (ed.), *Turkey and the West*, London, I.B.Tauris, 237–57.

———. (1995) "Islam and the Secular State in Turkey," in Çigdem Balım et al. (eds.), *Turkey: Political, Social and Economic Challenges in the 1990s*, Leiden, E. J. Brill, 90–96.

Toprak, Zafer. (1986) "1935 İstanbul Uluslararası Feminizm Kongresi ve Barış" (The 1935 International Istanbul Feminism Congress and Peace), *Toplum-Düşün*, 24, 24–29.

Toros, Elif. (2000) "Hayat, Hikayeler ve Suskunluğa Dair" (Concerning Life, Stories and Silence) in Yıldız Ramazanoğlu (ed.), *Osmanlı'dan*

Bibliography 143

*Cumhuriyet'e Kadının Tarihi Dönüşümü* (The Historical Transformation of Woman from the Ottoman Times to Our Day), İstanbul, Pınar Yayınları, 189–208.

Tuncer, Tuba. (1987) "Kimin aklı kısa?" (Whose brain is small?), *Zaman*, September 15.

Tura, Nesrin. (1997) "*Pazartesi* Neye Karşı" (What is *Pazartesi* Against), *Pazartesi*, 25, 6–7.

Turan, İlter. (1991) "Religion and Political Culture in Turkey," in R. L. Tapper (ed.), *Islam in Modern Turkey: Religion, Politics and Literature in a Secular State*, London, I.B.Tauris, 31–55.

Türkmen, Buket. (2000) "Laikliğin Dönüşümü: Liseli Gençler, Türban ve Atatürk Rozeti" (The Transformation of Secularism: High School Youth, Headscarf and the Ataturk Badge) in Nilüfer Göle (ed.), *İslamın Yeni Kamusal Yüzleri*, (The New Public Faces of Islam), İstanbul, Metis Yayınları, 110–47.

White, Jenny B. (1995) "Islam and Democracy: The Turkish Experience," *Current History*, 94/588, 7–12.

———. (1997) "Pragmatists or Ideologues? Turkey's Welfare Party in Power," *Current History*, 96/606, 25–30.

———. (2001) "The Islamist Movement in Turkey and Human Rights," *Human Rights Review*, 3/1, 17–26.

———. (2002) "The Islamist Paradox," in Deniz Kandiyoti and Ayşe Saktanber (eds.), *Fragments of Culture*, London, I.B.Tauris, 191–217.

———. (2002) *Islamist Mobilization in Turkey: A Study in Vernacular Politics*, Seattle, University of Washington Press.

Yavuz, Hakan. (1997) "Political Islam and the Welfare (Refah) Party in Turkey," *Comparative Politics*, 30/1, 63–82.

*Yeni Yüzyıl*. (1995) November 30.

*Yeni Yüzyıl*. (1998) September 25.

Zihnioğlu, Yaprak. (2003) *Kadınsız İnkılap* (Revolution Without Women), İstanbul, Metis yayınları.

## BROCHURES & POLITICAL PARTY PUBLICATIONS

Bayer, Handan. "İstanbul İl Hanımlar Komisyonu Çalışma Raporu"(Istanbul Province Ladies' Commission Work Report). September 3, 1997. Unpublished document.

Erbakan, Necmettin. *Türkiye'nin Meseleleri ve Çözümleri.* (Problems of Turkey and their Solutions), Ankara, Temmuz, 1991.

Erbakan, Necmettin. *Refah Partisi 4. Büyük Kongre, Açış Konuşması* (Welfare Party 4th Congress Opening Speech) October 10, 1993, Ankara: Gümüş matbaası.

*İstanbul 6. Olağan İl Kongresi Faaliyet Raporu* (6th Istanbul Province Ordinary Congress Activity Report).

*Milli Selamet Partisi Programı* (National Salvation Party Program). Ankara.

*Önce Ahlak ve Maneviyat* (First Morality and Morals) Refah Partisi, 1987.

*Refah Partisi Programı* (Welfare Party Program), Ankara.

*Refah Partisi 20 Ekim 1991 Genel Seçimi Seçim Beyannamesi* (Welfare Party October 20, 1991 General Elections Election Declaration).

*Refah Partisi 24 Aralık 1995 Seçimleri Seçim Beyannamesi* (Welfare Party December 24, 1995 General Elections Election Declaration).

*Refah Partisi 6. Olağan İl Kongresi Faaliyet Raporu*, İstanbul.

*Refah Partisi Ankara İl Teşkilatı 1993 Yılı Çalışma Programı* (Welfare Party Ankara Province 1993 Work Schedule)

*Refah Partisi İstanbul İl Teşkilatı 1990 Yılı Çalışma Programı* (Welfare Party Istanbul Province 1990 Work Schedule), İstanbul, 1990.

*Refah Partisi İstanbul İl Teşkilatı 1993 Çalışma Programı* (Welfare Party Istanbul Province 1993 Work Schedule).

*Teşkilat Rehberi, Refah Partisi* (Organization Guide, Welfare Party). October 1996.

*Women in Turkey,* General Directorate on the Status and Problems of Women, 1999, Ankara.

"Yükseköğretim Kurumlarında Kılık Kıyafet ile İlgili Mevzuat ve Hukuki Değerlendirmeler" (Statutes and Legal Judgments Concerning Dress Codes in Institutions of Higher Education). March 13, 1998, Council of Higher Education, Ankara.

# Index

activism:
of Refah Party women, 8–9;
women's, 11, 17
activist(s), 10–11, 45–46, 51, 71, 76,
78–79, 113;
female, 8–9, 17, 20, 68, 111, 113,
115, 119;
feminist, 17, 65;
Islamist, 58;
Islamist female, 109–110;
party, 46, 61;
Refah, 111;
woman, 53;
women, 1, 87
Adalet ve Kalkınma (Justice and
Development) Party, 1, 27
administrative council(s), 43–45, 47, 70
Aktaş, Cihan, 22–23, 125n20, 126n23,
127n34
Ankara, 12, 23, 32, 42–43, 45, 55, 57,
76–79, 85, 92–93;
organization, 46, 74;
Province Ladies' Commission, 74;
Provincial Organization, 42
Atatürk, Kemal, 7, 17–18, 29, 53, 55.
*See* Mustafa Kemal.
autonomy, 2, 33, 49–50, 54–55, 57–
58, 65, 87–88, 97–101, 114–116;
women's, 88, 102

Bulaç, Ali, 23, 54, 126n26
Bursa, 12

Çakır, Ruşen, 10–11, 122n18, 125n19,
126n24, 126n30

çarşaf, 61–62, 85, 87, 98
Çiftçi, Halise, 74, 76, 126n22
code(s), 4, 86;
civil (1926), 4, 15–16, 18, 28;
dress, 8, 24, 27, 85, 93, 105;
Islamic, 28;
Islamic legal, 15;
male Islamic dress, 4;
religious, 16, 106;
secular, 100, 103;
secular civil, 103
commission(s), 1, 40–44, 50–51, 55,
57, 62–66, 71–74, 79–87, 111–
112, 114, 118–119;
activities of, 44, 72;
members of, 42, 80, 82;
women in, 63, 74, 81, 109, 112;
women of, 66, 69, 75–80, 83–85,
111–113;
women's, 40
communitarianism, 6
Constitutional Court, 25–27, 39
Council of Higher Education, 24–25
cultural diversity, 2
custody, 15

democracy, 3–4, 9, 13, 17, 39, 89–90,
106–107, 109, 112, 114, 116;
liberal, 1–2, 108, 112–113, 115;
secular, 2
dentist(s), 50, 57, 98
Dilipak, Abdulrahman, 54
division of labor, 58, 95, 114, 118;
Islamist, 96–97;
traditional, 39, 95, 97–99, 120

145